Multiculturalism in Canada
Images and Issues

Barbara Samuels

Cheryl Craig

Weigl
CALGARY

KANATA
THE CANADIAN STUDIES SERIES

Eighth printing, 2003

Canadian Cataloguing in Publication Data

Samuels, Barbara A., 1949-
    Multiculturalism in Canada
    Includes index.
    ISBN 0-919879-69-1
    1. Multiculturalism–Canada. 2. Multiculturalism–Canada–History. I. Craig, Cheryl. II. Title.
FC104.S35 1995   305.8'00971   C95-910726-6
FC1035.A1S35 1995
This is a revised edition of Cultures in Canada by Norman Buchignani and Joan Engel. ©1983 Weigl Educational Publishers Limited.

Printed and bound in Canada for
Weigl Educational Publishers Limited
6325 - 10th Street S.E.
Calgary, Alberta   T2H 2Z9
Customer Service: 1-800-668-0766

Acknowledgements
We wish to acknowledge Dr. Norman E. Wagner, O.C., and his contribution to the development of this work. A special thank you is also extended to Dr. Ted Tetsuo Aoki for writing his own profile. The work of Dr. D. Jean Clandinin and Dr. F. Michael Connelly influenced the manner in which the notion of images is approached in this book.

Editor
Daniel Francis
Illustration and design
Warren Clark
Research and copy editing
Roberta Kuzyk-Burton, Janice Parker, Lauri Seidlitz, and Amanda Woodrow
Production
Warren Clark and Amanda Woodrow
Reviewer
Inez Farmer

Contents

Welcome To
Multiculturalism in Canada:
Images and Issues

This book is about Canadians. As you read it, you will learn that Canada is home to people from all over the world. You will find out when and why people chose Canada as their new home. You will see how Canada has grown and changed over time, and how Canadians have reacted to change. Former prime minister, Joe Clark, once called Canada "a community of communities." By this he meant that Canadian society is made up of different groups of people from different places with different backgrounds.

As you study *Multiculturalism in Canada: Images and Issues,* you will begin to understand how Canadians have met the challenge of living and working together. You will study examples of Canadians from varied backgrounds working side-by-side in harmony. You will also find that Canadians have not always respected the rights of other Canadians. Canadian history contains examples of tolerance, as well as of failures to live up to the ideal of treating one another fairly and equally.

Multiculturalism in Canada: Images and Issues explains what happened in the past, and how Canada became such a culturally-varied country. As you learn about the behaviour of people in the past, you will reflect on their actions. Did they treat others well or poorly? Although it is impossible to change what has already occurred, it is not too late to learn from our past.

Our ideas, policies, and viewpoints about multiculturalism have changed over time. *Multiculturalism in Canada: Images and Issues* examines the ways in which multiculturalism has been included in Canadian policies, and how government immigration and language policies have influenced the Canadian way of of life.

Images and Issues

This book asks you to think about Canada in terms of images and issues. Images reflect the way we make sense of experiences, both our own and those of other people. Images can also influence our behaviour. Sometimes, ideas we have about other people may be incomplete, and we run the risk of misunderstanding them. *Multiculturalism in Canada: Images and Issues* discusses many of the images that Canadians hold about Canada and about each other as citizens. This book explores how people's images shape and are shaped by their Canadian experiences.

Issues are the questions we ask ourselves about the kind of society we hope to create. Should Canada be a country of many cultures? What does this mean? Would it be better to have a single Canadian culture? What would that culture be like? These are all issues that you face as young people who will have an important role to play in the future of your country. *Multiculturalism in Canada: Images and Issues* helps you to explore these issues as they developed in the past and as they are debated in the present.

Using This Book

This book begins with an Introduction that looks at the ways in which multiculturalism affects you as an individual. It describes how different communities pass on their traditions from generation to generation. It also looks at the concepts of culture and multiculturalism. The Introduction asks you to think about some of the images that you have about the kind of country Canada is now, or should become in the future.

After the Introduction, the book is divided into three Units:

Unit 1, *Multiculturalism and You,* describes how different communities pass down their traditions from generation to generation. It also looks at some of the traditions valued by Canadian society.

Unit 2, *Multiculturalism and the Community,* explains how different communities have adapted to one another and to life in Canada.

Unit 3, *Multiculturalism and Canadian Policies,* explores government policies on immigration, multiculturalism, language rights, and human rights. These are the policies that create the kind of society in which Canadians wish to live.

Throughout the chapters, you will find a variety of case studies, activities, short biographies, and points of view that will help you expand your understanding of Canadian society. Each of these features is represented by an icon, or symbol.

Icons

 Key Terms

These are definitions that will help you understand important new words and concepts.

 Talk About

At the end of each chapter, this section is meant to encourage classroom discussion.

 Think About

This is a thought-provoking question or idea related to something you have read in the text.

 Questions

At the end of each chapter, and after some Case Studies and Profiles, questions ask you to recall and review what you have learned.

 Making Choices

When you see this icon, you will be asked to form your own opinion about an issue being discussed in the text.

 Quotations

Each chapter begins with a quotation relating to the subject of the chapter.

 Music Notes

Located throughout the chapters, music notes call attention to a piece of music that may call to mind a particular image of Canada.

PROFILE A brief overview of a person who has made, or is making, an important contribution to Canadian society.

CASE STUDY A detailed story about the challenges faced by individual Canadians as they adapt to life in Canada. Each Case Study highlights a particular issue facing Canadians.

VIEWPOINTS A collection of five different opinions about various issues raised in this book. Viewpoints help you to understand that there are always many opinions about any issue.

ACTIVITIES "Things to do" are located at the end of each chapter to assist you in understanding the ideas and issues about which you have been reading.

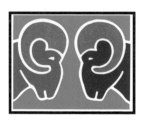

CHALLENGES are located at the end of each chapter. They challenge you to apply the main ideas of the chapter in special ways.

SKILL BUILDERS are located at the end of each chapter, providing an opportunity to use information to develop different skills.

Introduction

Images of Canada

When you are asked to describe Canada and its people, how do you respond? Most likely, you would begin by describing some of the ideas or images that come to mind when you think about the country.

No single image can possibly capture the essence of a place as large and diverse as Canada. However, over the years certain things have come to represent Canada for many people. A few examples of these things include the red maple leaf that adorns the Canadian flag, maple syrup, the game of hockey, the red uniform of the Mountie, the beaver, and the call of a loon on a northern lake.

Canada is the second-largest country in the world. When asked to describe it, we often think of its vast landscape: craggy Rocky Mountain peaks, the pounding sea of the Atlantic and Pacific coasts, the broad expanses of forest and lake, or the flat prairie stretching away to the horizon. All these features form images of the country.

> **Have you loved this land For what it is For its wealth Its freedom Its northern wind And above all For its people?**
>
> —Paul Call
> Canadian Poet

What images of Canada might each individual in this photograph have? Would you expect their images to be the same? Why? Why not?

Think About

When you think of Canada, what images fill your mind?

7

Canadians are as diverse as the geography of their country. For all their differences, Canadians share many values and traditions that are reflected in their country's institutions. For example, Canada is a democracy. We govern ourselves through representatives who we elect to serve us. As well, Canada has two official languages: French and English. Canadian laws uphold ideals such as individual rights and equality for all citizens. This means that all Canadians should have the same access to government services, and all should receive equal treatment before the law.

All these images and institutions represent different aspects of Canada. Taken together, they begin to describe the nature of Canadian culture.

What Is Culture?

Culture is a way of life shared by a group of people. It includes the knowledge they have, and all the things they do and make. It may be difficult to recognize your own culture because it is so much a part of your everyday life. Sometimes the best way to see your own culture is to compare it to someone else's. When you see people eating different foods, wearing different clothes, and educating their children in a different way, you suddenly recognize that there is a "Canadian" way of doing things as well.

Our history, our landscape, our sports, our holidays, our laws, and our government—all these things contribute to the Canadian way of life, to Canadian culture. No other country in the world is exactly like Canada, and no other people in the world are exactly like Canadians.

What Is Multiculturalism?

Canada is a country of new beginnings. That is why many people originally came to Canada—to start new lives. Some were fleeing oppression, others sought cheap land, and still more wanted an equal opportunity to get ahead. Whatever their reasons for coming, everyone thought that Canada offered a better way of life.

In the past, Canada relied on **immigrants** to fill its vast spaces and develop its many resources. As a result, it is natural for us to continue to extend a welcoming hand to new people. There is always a debate about how many newcomers it is wise to accept at any one time. Some Canadians believe Canada should continue to be a land of new Canadians. Others believe Canada has accepted enough newcomers in its history, and that our resources are best shared among the people who now live here.

Canada's mix of people can be compared to a large symphony

Key Term

A **culture** is a way of life shared by a group of people.

Immigrants are people who come from other countries to live in Canada.

orchestra. The bigger the orchestra, the harder it is to get everyone playing together, but the better the music sounds in the end. A fine orchestra is one in which all the different instruments are playing in harmony. It takes a good conductor and a lot of hard work to achieve harmony, but it can be done.

What makes a good member of the orchestra? First, each person should do what he or she does best. A drummer should not attempt to play the violin. Musicians need confidence in both themselves and in the instruments they play. Above all, they must practise until they play their instrument as well as they possibly can. Each member of the orchestra has an important role to play. The orchestra performs at its peak only when each member is playing his or her assigned part. They must get along as individuals to perform their best as a group.

Each instrument contributes to the success of the whole orchestra, just as each Canadian contributes to the success of the whole country.

Now think of Canadian society as a huge orchestra. There is great diversity between the different communities, just as there is great diversity between the strings and the horns and the percussion in the orchestra. Nevertheless, each section has an important part to play. When each is allowed to play its part, the "performance" is a smashing success.

If you take a bus tour through almost any city, you will see many examples of Canada's cultural diversity. You will see shops selling goods from different countries. On one corner you might see a delicatessen selling only smoked meats from Germany. Next to it there might be a restaurant selling English fish and chips, or Chinese food, or pizza from Italy. You might see a Native Friendship Centre, or a Hungarian community hall. Some parts of the city—Chinatown, for example—might have street signs in different languages. You will certainly see diverse places of worship: churches, synagogues, mosques, and temples devoted to many different religions.

All this variety is evidence that Canadian society consists of many cultures. It is what we mean when we say that Canada is a **multicultural** country.

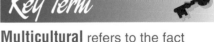

Key Term

Multicultural refers to the fact that Canada is a country of many different cultures.

Think About

Think about the part each person plays in making your school an important and interesting place to be. Does a country work the same way as your school? How?

9

Canada is the Rocky Mountains
Canada is Prince Edward Island
Canada is a country made for love
Canada is the prairie cowboy
Canada is the Yukon miner
Canada is a country made for love...
—from "Canada Is..."

Can you think of ways that will allow us to live in harmony as Canadians?

Racism occurs when people are not treated fairly because of their cultural or ethnic differences.

How Canadians Feel About Multiculturalism

Canada is a multicultural country; its citizens are of a wide variety of cultural backgrounds. However, there are many points of view about the impact multiculturalism has on Canadian society as a whole.

Many Canadians believe that diversity enriches Canadian culture. They believe that it is possible to be a strong Canadian, while at the same time remaining proud of a different cultural heritage. Other Canadians worry that Canada will not develop a strong national identity if members of all the different cultural communities hold on to their different cultural identities. They worry that multiculturalism divides instead of unites.

Other Canadians question the treatment received by visible cultural groups. We recognize visible cultural groups as different because of their physical appearance. By law, every Canadian has the same rights and privileges, but in daily life, people sometimes receive unfair treatment because of their cultural or ethnic differences. This is called **racism**.

The effect of racism is like one member of the orchestra playing the wrong notes, or refusing to play at all. For the sake of a harmonious performance, all the instruments must play together in tune. If we are going to live in harmony, everyone must be able to play their part.

Unit One

Multiculturalism and You

1 Keeping Up Traditions

Over the years, many people have come from other countries to create new lives for themselves in Canada. Some of these newcomers are recent arrivals; others have had family here for hundreds of years. You and your parents may have been born in Canada, but your grandparents may have come from another land. Everyone has his or her own personal history that can be traced back through time.

It is always interesting to find out about your family origins, and about what **traditions** you have kept through many generations. People who share the same traditions are often members of the same **ethnic group**.

What might you expect to find at the Passing of the Legends Museum in Exshaw, Alberta?

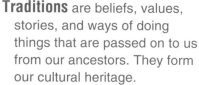

Traditions are beliefs, values, stories, and ways of doing things that are passed on to us from our ancestors. They form our cultural heritage.

An **ethnic group** is a group of people sharing the same traditions and the same background.

Storytellers pass on the traditions and values of a culture. Can you give an example of a story that does these things?

Traditions that are passed from generation to generation become part of a cultural heritage. Members of each new generation inherit the cultural heritage passed on to them by their ancestors. At the same time, they may adopt new traditions from other Canadians.

For example, you may celebrate the Chinese, Ukrainian, or Jewish New Year, but you may also celebrate New Year's Eve on December 31 of each year. If you are of Scottish heritage, you may take part in the Highland Games, but every July 1 you may also have a family picnic to celebrate Canada Day. At public gatherings, you may sing "O Canada" or "God Save the Queen," and at the same time you may have special stories and songs that mark festive occasions for you and your family. In this way, every culture is a mixture of old and new traditions.

One generation teaches the next about its traditions and customs, as well as its values and beliefs about life. This is how you learn what behaviour is acceptable, and how you should treat other people. For example, you learn that yelling at a rock concert is acceptable, but doing so at the symphony is not.

You learn these lessons from many people—from family, friends, teachers, writers, religious leaders, even from actors. Think about a film or television show with "good guys" and "bad guys." It is not hard to learn from these programs what behaviour is considered wrong.

Think About

When we celebrate Victoria Day or sing "God Save the Queen," what part of Canada's cultural heritage is being passed on to future generations?

13

Sharing Our Heritage

Traditions and customs pass from one generation to another in many ways. Many cultures around the world have important stories that are told in the form of legends, fables, and songs. Sometimes they are creation stories that explain how the world came to be. Other stories convey lessons about the proper way to behave. Children in different countries hear different versions of these stories. Each version reflects the values of the culture in which it is told.

Another way to pass on cultural traditions is through special ceremonies or celebrations. Canada has holidays marking important events. For example, Remembrance Day is celebrated every November 11 to honour the memories of the men and women who died in war defending an important Canadian cultural value—freedom. Poppies are worn out of respect for the lives that were lost. This annual event is a reminder of a significant piece of Canadian history, and reaffirms a fundamental Canadian value.

Perhaps you have been to a Bar Mitzvah (for a boy) or a Bat Mitzvah (for a girl). This is a ceremony that occurs when a boy or girl reaches the age when they are considered a full member of the Jewish community, ready to take on the responsibilities of adult Jewish life. Jewish people see the Bar or Bat Mitzvah as a link in a chain passing their beliefs, values, and customs from one generation to the next.

Cooking and clothing are also ways of passing on cultural traditions. Specially prepared foods such as tortière (meat pie), perogies (potatoes wrapped in dough), latkes (potato pancakes), Christmas cake, and schnitzel are all examples of foods that are associated with certain cultural groups. Your own family may have special foods that you have learned to make. Items of clothing or styles of dress are also part of a

The Jewish tradition of lighting the Sabbath candles is shared by two generations at a Bat Mitzvah.

person's cultural heritage. The things a cultural group chooses to pass on to its younger generation says a lot about what that culture considers to be important.

In Canada, one way in which **Aboriginal** People pass on their cultural heritage is through telling stories and singing songs about events that occurred in their past. Their stories and dances often feature the idea of a circle. To some Aboriginal Peoples, circles are important symbols. Among other things, they represent equality. When people sit in a storytelling circle, everyone is at the same level. There are no leaders and no followers. Each member of the group has an equally important part to play in the circle.

The Jewish passage into adulthood is celebrated by the community as a whole. For some Aboriginal groups, this rite of passage is private. The young person goes off on his or her own to fast and seek spiritual guidance. This is sometimes called a "Vision Quest." The young person is seeking a vision that will become a source of knowledge and strength throughout his or her adult life.

What values does the Vision Quest encourage? How does it compare to the traditions and values of other cultures that you know about?

The traditions that you inherit contribute to the kind of person you are. While some people want to maintain the traditions of their ancestors, others do not. Some traditions are considered to be outdated or impractical, and are replaced with new traditions. All Canadians, especially newcomers to the country, must find the right balance between old and new traditions.

Quentin Pipestem, a world champion hoop dancer, performs a dance based on a legend explaining life's difficulties and triumphs.

Key Term

Aboriginal refers to the original or earliest known inhabitants of a country. In the Canadian Constitution, the term Aboriginal Peoples refers to the Native, Métis, and Inuit peoples of Canada.

Language as an Expression of Culture

Why do you think French-speaking people in Québec and the rest of Canada are trying so hard to preserve their language?

Language is one of the most important cultural traditions passed from one generation to another. Learning to communicate with others vocally is one of the first things that children learn. A culture cannot survive without a common language in which its people can express themselves.

One of the biggest decisions that immigrants to a country like Canada must make is whether to continue using the language of

their ancestors. A common language strengthens cultural ties. Many people fear that losing their language is the first step in losing their culture. Yet Canadians must be able to communicate with one another if they hope to live in harmony. No country can function well if everyone speaks a different language. Imagine what it would be like if we could not understand one another when we spoke. You may wish to role-play this situation with a classmate. Think back to the example of the orchestra. If one of the instruments is playing a different tune, listeners will not understand what they are hearing.

Canada has two official languages— French and English. Canadian law states that Canada is a **bilingual** country. Canadians are expected to speak either French or English or both. Individuals may keep the language of their ancestors if they wish, as long as they also adopt one or both of the official languages of the country.

Canada made a commitment to both English and French languages through the *Official Languages Act* in 1969. The Canadian government carries out this commitment through efforts like the Heritage Languages program, a program that helps immigrant children learn English or French, and other skills they need to be able to function well in Canadian society.

Recently, other cultural groups have asked to have support for their languages and traditions. One example is a Ukrainian encyclopedia that was published on behalf of the Canadian Foundation for Ukrainian Studies. The Foundation believes that it is important for Ukrainians in Canada to preserve their language and heritage, and that the encyclopedia will help their effort to do so.

Bilingual is the ability to speak two languages.

Why are publications such as the Ukrainian encyclopedia so important to all Canadians?

Learning to Live in Canada

When people from other cultures settle in Canada, they bring their own customs, their own ideas, and their own ways of doing things. As the years pass, they continue with the old ways that are familiar and important to them. At the same time, they learn new, "Canadian" ways of doing things. In some cases, they give up the old ways in favour of new ideas that seem to work better in their new country. This exchange of ideas and customs goes on continuously between newcomers to Canada and the people who are already living here. The exchange keeps Canadian culture vibrant and interesting.

Read about the changes experienced by members of the Wan family since they came to Canada.

The Wans are committed to hard work, their community, and their family. Kin-Kong Wan, the father of six children, has two dental clinics in Vancouver's Chinatown. He works long hours at his practice, which is open from 9 am to 7 pm, six days a week. These hours are unusual for a dentist office, but it is a Chinatown tradition to provide service in the evening and on Saturday. According to Dr. Wan, being a workaholic is a Hong Kong tradition. He has a large family to support, including his mother, brother, and three sisters who still live in Hong Kong. He says he does not feel comfortable unless he is working.

Kin-Kong Wan was born in China, and moved to Hong Kong when he was eight years old. At this point his family became separated. His father and some of his brothers and sisters remained behind in China. Kin-Kong Wan and

The Wans brought ideas and values with them when they came to Canada. Have they had to sacrifice any of them to become Canadian?

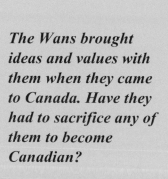

his mother were very poor in Hong Kong. She ran a small shop where he worked after school until midnight every night. When the shop closed, he put a board on top of the refrigerator and slept there. Getting an education was the most important thing in Kin-Kong Wan's life. He was determined to get into university. He hoped to become a doctor, but by age fourteen he knew his marks were not good enough to meet the very high standards of the Hong Kong medical school. Instead, Kin-Kong Wan set his sights on dentistry. His family borrowed money to send him to Canada where other friends were studying. He enrolled at the University of Toronto and promptly took three jobs to pay his way through school.

After his studies, Kin-Kong Wan chose to remain in Canada rather than return to Hong Kong. He preferred the stability and the slower pace of life here.

The Wan family now lives in a neighbourhood of many different ethnic groups on the east side of Vancouver, near Dr. Wan's clinics. Family photographs, sports trophies, and a huge mural of peacocks decorate the walls of their home, along with a ceramic Buddha tucked away on the top shelf of a bookcase. The Buddha is just a nod to tradition since neither Kin-Kong Wan nor his wife Lisa Wan practise the Buddhist religion. They enjoy living in the city. They were accustomed to more crowded conditions. They like the convenience of being in town, as well as the fact that living together with other Chinese Canadians fosters a spirit of community. Their community provides a choice of Chinese radio stations, movie theatres, two pay-TV channels, several daily newspapers, and a complete range of shopping, financial, and medical services.

Living in a Chinese community does not give the Wans much chance to improve their English, but they are working toward getting better command of the language. Kin-Kong Wan is a member of the Toastmasters Club, where he practises public speaking, and he has joined a number of other groups in order to "improve himself." Lisa Wan has done the same. She takes singing lessons and skates, swims and plays racquetball for exercise. The Wans also jog and ski.

Lisa Wan does not want to be a full-time homemaker, but she treads a careful path between a traditional and a modern marriage. She believes that in many ways she is a traditional Chinese woman who leaves everything to her husband to decide. In other ways, she fights for the "Canadian way." "I have Canadian ideas," she says. "I want to start my own business." Yet she has to struggle with the knowledge that her husband will not accept it.

Chinese families place a high value on scholarship. Kin-Kong Wan expects his children to perform well at school and to value their education. As far as he is concerned, A is good, B is pass, and C is failure—forget the school's grading system. One of his daughters, Victoria Wan, notes that she has absorbed some of her family's Chinese values. Most of her friends are Asian, and she has chosen them according to her exacting standards. They must be hard-working, trustworthy, fun-loving, and honest. At the same time, Victoria Wan believes that a career is important, and wants to be independent. The old-fashioned notion of a subservient wife is not for her. Lisa Wan approves of her children's Western values. "They are Canadian born, that's the way they think and act. That's fine. This is Canada."

Questions

1. What are some of the ways the Wans have adapted to the Canadian way of life? How has it changed their family?
2. What traditional Chinese values and traditions have the Wans passed on to their children?
3. Should the Wans encourage their children to adopt Canadian customs? Why or why not?

Tracing Your Roots

Do you know where your parents, grandparents, or great-grandparents were born? If you drew a family tree showing all the places where members of your family originated, you might be surprised to discover that they came from many different countries. Like Canada itself, your family might be multicultural. This is because most families do not have a single cultural heritage.

If you compare your family tree to others in the class, you will discover that it is completely unique. No family history is the same as any other. By discovering and recording your family history, you are involved in the study of **genealogy**.

Arrange to interview one or more of your family members. Keep a journal of their responses. Here are some questions you may wish to ask:

- In what country were you born? What was life like there when you were young?
- Why did you come to Canada? What did you expect to find? Were your expectations met?
- What traditions from the Old World did you keep? What traditions did you adopt as a Canadian?

Decide on the shape of your family tree. What will the branches look like? How many different cultures can you find in your background?

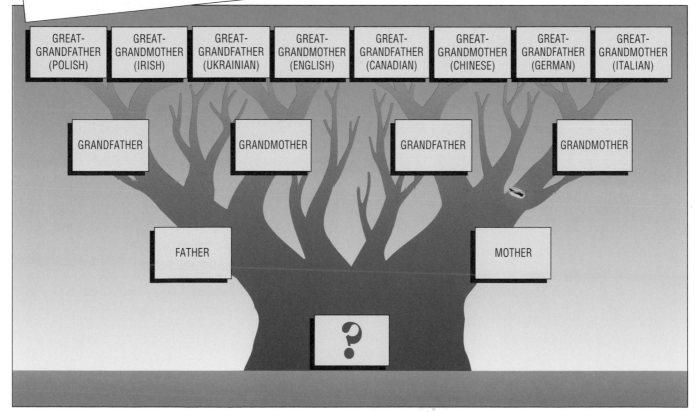

| GREAT-GRANDFATHER (POLISH) | GREAT-GRANDMOTHER (IRISH) | GREAT-GRANDFATHER (UKRAINIAN) | GREAT-GRANDMOTHER (ENGLISH) | GREAT-GRANDFATHER (CANADIAN) | GREAT-GRANDMOTHER (CHINESE) | GREAT-GRANDFATHER (GERMAN) | GREAT-GRANDMOTHER (ITALIAN) |

GRANDFATHER   GRANDMOTHER   GRANDFATHER   GRANDMOTHER

FATHER   MOTHER

?

What is in a Name?

An important clue to your cultural background may be found in your last, or family, name. Traditionally, family names, or surnames, are passed down through the father to his sons and daughters. Until recently, most Canadian women took the family name of the men they married. This tradition has changed over the past few years. Today some women choose to keep their maiden name (their family name before marriage), rather than adopt the family name of their husband. Other women choose to hyphenate their last name so that it includes both their maiden name and their husband's name.

Names are as individual as signatures. They identify who you are, and they may be a revealing link to your ancestors. The common practice in Canada is to

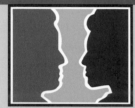

Theoren Fleury

Theoren Fleury, member of the Calgary Flames hockey team, traces his surname to his Métis roots. One of Theoren's great-great-grandfathers was born of a French father and a Cree mother in 1883 in Fort Rouge, once a French fur trading fort, and now part of Winnipeg.

On his mother's side, Theoren's grandparents were of German and French/English backgrounds.

Theoren's mother, Donna, whose surname before marriage was Lario, grew up in Oxbow, Saskatchewan. Theoren's father, Wally, grew up in a Métis settlement on the banks of the Assiniboine River near St. Lazare, Manitoba. About one hundred people from about ten Métis

families who were related lived on a quarter section of land originally settled by Wally's great-grandfather. According to Theoren's father, this settlement followed many Métis traditions, such as addressing one another with nicknames, and maintaining close-knit families and neighbourhoods. This land has now become part of a Métis land claim.

Theoren's father is active in Métis organizations. He has been

a Representative to the Métis Senate, and is currently the chairperson of the Pelly Trail local Métis Association and the chairperson of the Southwest Region of Manitoba Métis.

Theoren was born in Oxbow, Saskatchewan, in 1968. Theoren, like his youngest brother Travis, was named after a character in the film, *Old Yeller*. Theoren's younger brother, Theodore (Ted), was named after one of their mother's grandfathers.

Theoren's family and life story, like that of many Canadians, presents a diverse ancestry.

Questions

1. Can you rely on a person's name as a clue to their ancestry? Why or why not?
2. Research what your first name means. Where does your name originate from?

give children a first name, one or more middle names, and a family name. Your first and middle names may also reflect your cultural heritage. If you look around your class, you will see that there are many names that reflect cultural heritages.

Different cultures have different ways of choosing names. In parts of Africa, for example, names sometimes stand for the time of day a person was born, the order of birth, or some important family event. Jewish children have two first names: a Hebrew name not used in everyday life, and a more common Canadian name. A male child's Hebrew name also tells us who his father is. Roman Catholics often name their children after saints or other religious figures. Turkish, Slavic, and Russian names often reflect national pride. After arriving in Canada, new immigrants often choose new "Canadian" first names.

In Europe many centuries ago, only nobles had family, or "sir," names. The word "surname" comes from this early time. Later, surnames tended to become nicknames, chosen because of a person's appearance, habits, or occupation. If your name was Smith, Baker, or Taylor, what might your ancestors' occupation have been? Can you think of some other examples? What about your own name? Do you know where it came from?

There may also be special meaning in the names of cities, towns, rivers, and villages. Some places are named after people,

I have heard the wild wind sing the places that I have been,
Bay Bull and Red Deer and Strait of Belle Isle,
Names like Grand Mère and Silverthrone, Moose Jaw and Marrowbone,
Trails of the pioneer, named with a smile.

—from "Something to Sing About"

This house once belonged to Arthur Wellesley, the Duke of Wellington, a famous British war hero. It is located in a town now called Wellington, Ontario.

others are named after an interesting feature of the town, and still others are named in languages that reflect the heritage of the original settlers. Place names can tell a lot about who lived there and where they came from.

Take the city of Calgary, for example. In the Gaelic language, Calgary, or Cala-ghearridh, means "preserved pasture at the harbour," or "bay farm." A Colonel from the North-West Mounted Police, James Macleod, suggested the name of Calgary. Some people believe that Colonel Macleod chose the name because he had once visited Calgary Bay on the Isle of Mull in Scotland, and that the valley between the Bow and Elbow rivers resembled the Scottish countryside of the Isle of Mull.

The name of your own community might have a special meaning. Do some research to find out where the name originated. What do the origins of the name reveal about the history of the community? You can do the same for a street name, the name of your school, a park, or a nearby landmark.

Think About

If you were asked to name a person, a place, or even a street, what name would you choose in each case? Why did you choose the name you did?

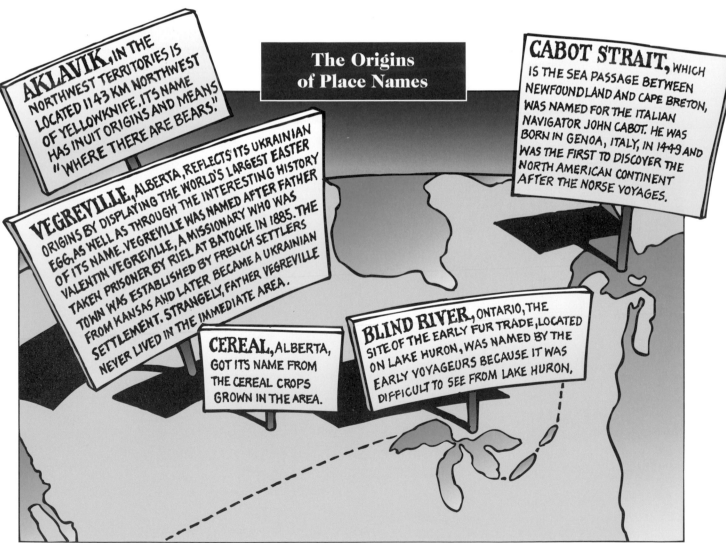

The Origins of Place Names

AKLAVIK, IN THE NORTHWEST TERRITORIES IS LOCATED 1143 KM NORTHWEST OF YELLOWKNIFE, ITS NAME HAS INUIT ORIGINS AND MEANS "WHERE THERE ARE BEARS."

VEGREVILLE, ALBERTA, REFLECTS ITS UKRAINIAN ORIGINS BY DISPLAYING THE WORLD'S LARGEST EASTER EGG, AS WELL AS THROUGH THE INTERESTING HISTORY OF ITS NAME. VEGREVILLE WAS NAMED AFTER FATHER VALENTIN VEGREVILLE, A MISSIONARY WHO WAS TAKEN PRISONER BY RIEL AT BATOCHE IN 1885. THE TOWN WAS ESTABLISHED BY FRENCH SETTLERS FROM KANSAS AND LATER BECAME A UKRAINIAN SETTLEMENT. STRANGELY, FATHER VEGREVILLE NEVER LIVED IN THE IMMEDIATE AREA.

CEREAL, ALBERTA, GOT ITS NAME FROM THE CEREAL CROPS GROWN IN THE AREA.

BLIND RIVER, ONTARIO, THE SITE OF THE EARLY FUR TRADE, LOCATED ON LAKE HURON, WAS NAMED BY THE EARLY VOYAGEURS BECAUSE IT WAS DIFFICULT TO SEE FROM LAKE HURON.

CABOT STRAIT, WHICH IS THE SEA PASSAGE BETWEEN NEWFOUNDLAND AND CAPE BRETON, WAS NAMED FOR THE ITALIAN NAVIGATOR JOHN CABOT. HE WAS BORN IN GENOA, ITALY, IN 1449 AND WAS THE FIRST TO DISCOVER THE NORTH AMERICAN CONTINENT AFTER THE NORSE VOYAGES.

Ted Tetsuo Aoki

Sometimes Canadians and people who become Canadians change their names. They do this for a variety of reasons. Perhaps they think their name is too hard for other Canadians to pronounce or to spell. Perhaps they feel a new name will help them "fit in better."

Ted Tetsuo Aoki, a well-known educator, has undergone many name changes in his life. Born Tetsuo Aoki, he was known as Ted during his school years. Later he preferred to be called Tetsuo, but now he goes by Ted. His official signature is Ted Tetsuo Aoki.

Here is how Ted Tetsuo Aoki describes the quest for identity that underlies his name changes:

Born in British Columbia of Japanese parents, I found myself placed in an ethnic category called "Japanese Canadian." In my school years, having attended two schools daily, I became somewhat bilingual and bicultural, speaking both English and Japanese.

I have always been puzzled by the label "Japanese Canadian" that seemingly identified me in multicultural Canada as a member of a minority ethnic group. Puzzled, I began to ask, "Who am I?"—a question that has obsessed me for many years. Told that my

identity is rooted in my heritage, I even visited Japan several times in search of who I am.

Although I learned much about Japan and the Japanese, the answer to the question of identity, "Who am I as a Japanese Canadian?" continued to escape me, as it escapes me even today.

I wonder. Could it be that I have long been deluded into believing that my identity is something present, but hidden and discoverable? Or could it be that what I call my identity is not so much found, as something crafted in the midst of my life with others, my fellow Canadians? I continue to wonder and to ponder.

Today, I am beginning to think that what is called my Japanese "Canadianess" is both discovered and crafted.

Making Choices ✓

1. How do Ted Tetsuo Aoki's name changes reflect his questions about his identity?
2. Decide what Dr. Aoki is saying about Canadian identity.
3. Do you agree with his argument that a person's identity is both discovered and crafted? Explain.

Keeping Score

Statistics Canada, an agency within the federal government, keeps track of many facts about Canadians. Statistics Canada is like the nation's scorekeeper. It uses surveys and questionaires to find the answers to many questions.

Usually every five years, Statistics Canada conducts a survey asking each household in the country to answer a number of questions describing itself. These questions include: how many people live in your home? what occupations do they have? how much money do they make? what language did they first learn to speak? what level of schooling do they have? This large survey is called a **census**. Among other things, a census provides the official population count of the country.

In its 1991 census, Statistics Canada reported some interesting information. It asked all Canadians to report their cultural heritage. The following chart shows how people replied to the question.

The 1991 census showed that a growing number of people report that their cultural heritage is Canadian. Do you think this number will continue to grow? Why? Why not?

What Canadians said about their Cultural Heritage

Canada	Number	%
Total Population	26 994 045	100.0
Single responses	19 199 795	71.1
1. French	6 146 605	22.8
2. British	5 611 050	20.8
3. German	911 560	3.4
4. Canadian	765 095	2.8
5. Italian	750 055	2.8
6. Chinese	586 645	2.2
7. Aboriginal	470 615	1.7
8. Ukrainian	406 645	1.5
9. Dutch (Netherlands)	358 185	1.3
10. East Indian	324 840	1.2

Source: Statistics Canada

Key Term

A **census** is a statistical survey of a population. It is usually an official survey done by the government. In Canada, census information is collected every five years. Because it has to be tabulated, the information does not reach the public for a few years after that. As a result, the statistics are always somewhat out-of-date. A census contains much information that helps people to understand trends in the population.

In 1969, only 69 000 people reported that they were of Canadian heritage. This compares to 765 095 people in the 1991 census, which is eleven times more. The comparison shows that more and more people, regardless of where they were born, are reporting that their cultural heritage is Canadian. The change from the census carried out in 1969 is quite astonishing. Apparently Canadians are changing the way they think about themselves and their country.

Is there a Canadian culture?

We should be proud of our ancestors. By using terms such as Chinese Canadian, Italian Canadian, Ukrainian Canadian, and so on, we recognize our heritage and background.

It's about time we recognized that we have a real culture here in Canada—a Canadian culture. We have Canadian customs and traditions, and we are different from other nations of the world.

I don't believe that just because a person has Italian, German, Dutch, or other ethnic genes, it automatically determines a person's culture. Culture is more than biology. You are shaped by your experiences.

We will never become a strong and united country until we agree that we are all Canadians. We must be proud of our country, whether we were born here or whether it has become our adopted home.

We know what we are as Canadians by what we are not. We know we are not Americans. We know we are not British.

Decide the viewpoint that best matches your own. Argue for or against any of the viewpoints. Make a list of the arguments you will make.

What We Have Learned

Canada's history can be traced backwards in time. So can the history of each individual living in Canada. These histories include traditions that are passed from one generation to the next, traditions that help to define our culture. Culture is passed on through language, names, stories, songs, and celebrations. For people who originally came from other countries and who now call Canada home, some traditions may have changed over time, and other traditions may have been preserved. Sometimes traditions change for newcomers as a result of how living in Canada has influenced their way of life. Taken together, all of these elements form Canadian culture—or what we have come to call multicultural Canada.

Talk About

When families from different cultural backgrounds move to Canada, how difficult is it for them to adjust to a new way of life? How big of a gap is there between them and their neighbours, friends, fellow workers, and even their own children, who have been exposed to new ideas and influences?

Questions

1. What is culture?
2. How is Canadian culture passed on?
3. What is a census and why is it important?
4. Why is language important to the survival of a culture?
5. What is the main purpose of the *Official Languages Act*?

Activities

1. Invite visitors to the classroom to discuss their views on multiculturalism. Try to find people with differing points of view.
2. Visit a cultural group in your community other than your own. Possible places to visit include a cultural centre, a museum, or a place of worship. What did your visit teach you about the cultural group? Discuss the advantages of living in a culturally diverse community.
3. In Québec, many people celebrate St. Jean Baptiste Day. Find out more about this holiday and what it celebrates. What part of Québec's cultural heritage does this holiday pass on?

Challenges

1. Actors and performers sometimes take on "stage" names. Why do you think they change their names? Do you know anyone who has changed his or her name? Find out what has to be done to change a name in your province.
2. Using a map that shows all the cities and towns in your province, make a list of ten interesting place names that reflect a variety of cultural origins. Can you guess where each name came from? Choose one of the names on your list. Write to the Chamber of Commerce in that town or city to find out the real story behind the name.
3. As a class, take a census of the school. What questions will you ask?
4. Write about a day in your life. Can you identify the cultural origins of some of the things that you do each day?

Skill Builders

1. Using a wall map of the world, locate and list your classmates' and teachers' countries of origins.
2. Use your graph-making skills to prepare a series of four bar graphs depicting information gathered from your family trees. The four graphs will have these titles:
   - We Were Born in These Countries
   - Our Parents Were Born in These Countries
   - Our Grandparents Were Born in These Countries
   - Our Great-grandparents Were Born in These Countries
3. Imagine you are a songwriter. Write new lyrics to a familiar song. Add interesting Canadian place names.
4. Use your artistic skills to make a poster expressing different feelings about multiculturalism. Clip newspaper articles that illustrate people's various viewpoints on this subject.

2 Valuing the Individual

J ust as the conductor of an orchestra values each instrument for the part it plays in the overall symphony, multiculturalism values the contribution each individual makes to society as a whole.

Canada is a country that was built by many people from many different countries and cultural backgrounds. One of the main goals of multiculturalism is to encourage respect for every individual's lifestyle, to be fair, and to treat everyone equally. Canadian laws discourage prejudice, discrimination, stereotyping, and racism.

Have you ever wondered what the words prejudice, stereotyping, discrimination, and racism really mean? Would you recognize when they happened?

Prejudice is a feeling and an attitude. If you have bad opinions about someone, or some group, before you really know anything about them, you are pre-judging them. Prejudice happens when opinions about all members of a group are based on the actions of just a few members of that group. Imagine, for example, that you saw a few teenagers shouting at someone and calling them names. If you then decided that this is the way all teenagers behave, and if you assumed that the next teenager you met was going to be equally rude and unruly, you would be prejudiced against teenagers. You would be pre-judging all teenagers based on the behaviour of a few.

A **stereotype** is a belief about a person, or a group, that does not take into account individual differences. A stereotype becomes frozen in your mind, and stops you from thinking of individuals as unique, different, or special. Based on your experience with the rude teenagers, you might make up your mind about all teenagers before you got to know any of them. You would then have a stereotype about teenagers: "they are all rude and wild." You might treat teenagers differently based on this stereotype. You would have allowed the actions of a few individuals to colour your attitude toward an entire group.

Have you ever seen a sign in a restaurant that said "Teenagers Not Served Here"? Or been in a store where the clerks did not serve teenagers with the same eagerness as they did adults? The owners of

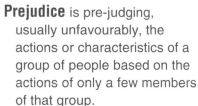

Key Term

Prejudice is pre-judging, usually unfavourably, the actions or characteristics of a group of people based on the actions of only a few members of that group.

A **stereotype** is a belief about a person or group of people that does not recognize individual differences.

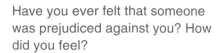

Think About

Have you ever felt that someone was prejudiced against you? How did you feel?

The Canadian Charter of Rights and Freedoms document contains the following sections:

CANADIAN CHARTER OF RIGHTS AND FREEDOMS

Guarantee of Rights and Freedoms

Fundamental Freedoms

Democratic Rights

Mobility Rights

Legal Rights

Equality Rights

Official Languages of Canada

Minority Language Educational Rights

Enforcement

General

Application of Charter

Citation

these businesses may have already formed a stereotype about teenagers because of some teenagers who had caused trouble in the past. The way that teenagers are treated by the owners is a form of **discrimination**.

Discrimination occurs when a person behaves negatively toward someone else because of prejudice and stereotypes. In our example, the owners are discriminating against teenagers by refusing to serve them and by treating them differently than other customers.

When you pick a book from the library to read, you usually choose something by a favourite author or on a favourite subject. In other words, you make a choice. You discriminate between authors, or between subjects that interest you. However, these choices are not harmful to other people. Discrimination becomes harmful when your choices, and your actions, are rooted in prejudice.

This is the Canadian Charter of Rights and Freedoms. Why is it important that the Charter guarantees equal rights for all citizens?

Key Term

Discrimination is behaviour that is based on prejudiced attitudes and beliefs.

Celebrating Cultural Heritage

In Calgary, one group of Canadians uses Black History Month as an opportunity to discuss their cultural heritage and to explore stereotypes. Why have they chosen to do so?

When Genevieve Balogun's son studied history in Grade 9, he decided to do a project on an Arctic explorer. There was nothing unusual in that, except the explorer he chose was Matthew Henson, a Black who ventured to the North Pole in 1909 with Robert Peary.

Balogun is president of the Calgary chapter of the Congress of Black Women, which organizes Black History Month in Calgary. She says the month is important "because it reminds us of our rich history that is so often lost in the shuffle." It is a chance, especially for the younger generation, to celebrate the accomplishments of Blacks. Everyone from Martin Luther King Jr., the American civil rights leader, to George Washington Carver, the inventor of peanut butter, is recognized.

"It's an excuse to have fun, too, I won't pretend otherwise," Balogun adds with a gust of laughter.

Balogun works hard to make sure that February is fun. She arranges something almost every day of the month, from Caribbean cooking classes, artistic events, and job seminars, to special church services and a youth conference on staying in school.

The idea behind all the events is to celebrate the diversity of Blacks in Calgary, and to bring the values of different cultures together. Balogun points out that Black Africans have a very different culture from Blacks who grew up in Caribbean countries, and from those raised in the United States.

"We have in common our skin colour, but our background and experiences are very different," she says. "We are Canadians first and foremost, but we have brought our heritage with us and we can't leave it behind."

Balogun sees Black History Month as an opportunity for the Black community to talk about their experiences and explore stereotypes about themselves.

Questions

1. Why is it important to recognize the achievements of different cultures through special events such as Black History Month? Can you think of other examples?
2. What accomplishments of Black people can you list?

How Racism Develops

Prejudice or discrimination against people of a particular race or ethnic background is called racism. Groups that are the target of racism are often not allowed to participate fully in society because of the prejudice against them.

A well-known example of racism is the way in which many white Americans used to treat Blacks. In the American South, Blacks were not allowed to mingle with whites. Their schools were separate; they were not even allowed to go to the same restaurants. When they travelled on buses, Blacks had to sit in the back. The laws did not change until civil rights leaders such as Martin Luther King Jr. challenged them in the 1950s and 1960s.

Racism sometimes flares up when new immigrants come to a country. People sometimes think that immigrants, who often speak different languages and have different customs, are competing for jobs and housing with people who are already in the country. Some feel the immigrants threaten "the order of things." Every year, for example, about 250 000 immigrants arrive in Canada. There are legitimate arguments to be made both for and against accepting this many newcomers. Many people feel that the economy and society cannot absorb so many new people at once. Others argue the opposite, that immigrants contribute much more to the country than they cost.

Sometimes, however, the debate targets immigrants as the cause of economic and social problems. If people have trouble finding jobs, for example, they may blame it on competition from the newcomers. It is when these attitudes harden into prejudice against the newcomers, who are singled out because of their skin colour or cultural background, that racism may result.

Some forms of racism can be dealt with by laws that protect people from racist behaviour. It is illegal, for example, to refuse to rent an apartment to someone because of their skin colour. Most provinces have Human Rights Commissions to deal with complaints of discrimination and racism.

However, racism is an attitude and it is hard to change attitudes with laws. Some forms of racism are so subtle that laws cannot deal with them. Sometimes people are even guilty of racism without realizing it. The real key to ending racism and discrimination is to learn to treat all people with respect and dignity. Canadian schools, cities, community groups, clubs, and hospitals participate each year in the International Day for the Elimination of Racial Discrimination.

Racism is an emotional issue. When members of a group feel that they are not being allowed to participate fully in society, they sometimes protest to draw attention to their concerns.

Think About

How do you think stereotypes and racist attitudes develop? What can we do to prevent their growth?

Making Choices

Imagine you are with a group of people eating lunch, and you hear racist comments being made about a classmate. How would you respond?

The Girl in the Hall

Danielle Gallant, a thirteen-year-old student at St. Stephen's High, Stephenville, Newfoundland, wrote this story based on her own experience. Danielle questioned her actions after witnessing an example of discrimination in her school. What would you have done in her place?

It was on a morning in November when I saw for the first time the new girl with the olive complexion and curly black hair. She wore a long flowered skirt and an obviously very aged white blouse. She crept slowly down the hall with an air of uncertain hesitation about her. As she walked, she kept her back against the hard tiles of the wall as if she wanted to remain as inconspicuous, as unnoticeable, as she could. With each step a small, brown foot peeped out from under her skirt and I could see that all she wore on her feet were a pair of worn leather sandals.

I could tell that she was new to our town, this girl with the strange clothes, because when she approached a teacher and spoke to him, the words were not familiar to me. The few recognizable words she did speak were thick and slurred. The teacher did not understand. I could see that right away, and the girl sank back towards the locker with an embarrassed look on her face.

Suddenly, a loud giggle pierced the air. A few lockers away, a group of people had formed. It was easy to see that they were laughing at the new girl. I looked her way to see if she had noticed, but she just turned away.

Gradually, a group of students gathered around the girl. By now, the first bell had rung and the girl was clearly confused. No one seemed to notice or care. All they noticed was that dark skin, those big black eyes, and those funny clothes. The crowd became bolder and bolder. The muffled giggles grew into outright laughter and now there wasn't an eye in the hall that wasn't focussed on the unfortunate girl.

I looked away. I couldn't stand to see her face. I couldn't look at her, knowing how much she must be hurting. I wanted to help her, wanted to stand up for her. More than anything, I wanted to tell these people how wrong they were, how cruel they were being. I wanted to make them feel as badly as she must have been feeling.

Instead, I just stood there. I was scared to say anything. Scared that these people would tease and laugh at me, just as they teased and laughed at her.

Finally I forced myself to look at her face. Written there I saw all the pain and anger I knew I would see, but there was something else, something I hadn't expected. Her expression revealed a clearly defined look of acceptance as if she had expected this, and had decided that she must put up with it. I knew then that none of this was new to her; she had seen it all before. The whispering, the laughter, the teasing, it was all the same to her.

Voices began to rise out of the crowd. I could hear the jokes, the insults, and I knew she could too. I glanced over at her and saw that despite the fact that she spoke a different language, she understood what they were saying. There are some things that run deeper than words. They are part of an international language, understood by all people, no matter who, no matter where.

The second bell rang and the hall cleared. Only the girl and I remained. Suddenly she turned and I

Why do you think the group treated the girl in the hall the way they did?

found myself looking into sparkling black eyes that were overflowing with tears. I shivered, conscious of the uncanny feeling that this girl with her penetrating gaze knew what I was thinking.

A feeling of guilt washed over me. I'd had the chance to help this girl. I could have been a friend when she needed one. But I hadn't. I had done nothing.

I turned away and began to walk down the hall. I told myself that it wasn't my fault and that it wasn't my responsibility to stick up for her. But somehow, I couldn't remove the feeling that I had, in some way, treated her just as the others had. I was as bad as they were.

I glanced over my shoulder, only to see her still standing there. She looked at me and I could tell she wanted my help. I turned away and walked down the hall. I didn't look back.

Danielle's story is about one person's feelings after seeing someone ridiculed for being different. Danielle believed that the group of students was doing something wrong. She believed that she had also done something wrong by failing to stick up for the new girl. The fact that Danielle felt uncomfortable and unhappy about what happened shows that she is beginning to rethink her behaviour.

Questions

1. What could the girl in the hall do to stop this type of treatment by her classmates?
2. How might Danielle have acted differently?
3. Write another ending to Danielle's story, or write about a similar incident from your own experience.

Does Canada have a problem with racism?

If I were a landlord, I should have every right to rent to anyone I want. Why should the government have the right to tell me who I can rent to?

My swimming club is very selective about its membership. We're a private club. Why should we let everyone join?

We shared great stories and swapped recipes with the students in my community. They have come to Canada and are now Canadian citizens. We sure can learn a lot from others.

If I had my own company, I would never offer immigrants a job. They might not fit in with my other workers.

I believe we are doing everything we can in Canada to stamp out racism. We have laws and Human Rights Commissions to deal with complaints.

Making Choices ✓

Talk about whether Canada has a problem with racism. Does your community? Does your school? Debate the issue.

Appreciating the Value of the Individual

An equal, fair society does not promote racism and discrimination. It respects individual differences, and recognizes the special contributions all people can make.

One way to show appreciation for individual contributions is by honouring people with awards. The conductor of an orchestra will ask the soloist, and then the other musicians, to take a bow at the end of a piece of music so that the audience can show its appreciation for their performance. Individual Canadians are sometimes honoured for their hard work and success, especially when their achievements have resulted in a better way of life for other Canadians.

There are many ways that recognition and honours are given. Do you have a trophy or certificate on the shelf at home? Whether it is from your little league team, your karate class, your band, your dance competition, or your school, it is perhaps something that you cherish because others have recognized and congratulated you on your hard work or your special talents.

Awards are sometimes given by a country. On July 1, 1967, on the 100th anniversary of Canada's Confederation, the government created an award, called the Order of Canada, to honour Canadians who have enriched the lives of others. There are three levels of membership for the Order of Canada: Companion, Officer, and Member. The Companion level is given for international achievement; the Officer level for national achievement; and the Member level for contributions at the local or regional level. Recipients may use special letters after their names to indicate their status: CC (Companion of the Order), OC (Officer of the Order), or CM (Member of the Order). Recipients are also given a badge and ribbons representing the order to wear on special occasions, and a small pin to wear with everyday clothes. The badge and pin are made up of a snowflake, a crown, a maple leaf, and a Latin motto meaning "They desire a better country."

Other awards that attract much attention nationally are the Governor General's Literary Awards, which are given out annually to recognize and reward Canadian writers. These awards are given to the English- and French-language works that are selected as the best in each of the following six categories: fiction, non-fiction, drama, poetry, children's literature, and translation. Winners receive a medal from the Governor General, $10 000, and a specially-bound copy of their award-winning work.

Above is the seal of the Order of Canada and below is a badge of a Companion of the Order of Canada. The motto on the badge, "Desiderantes meliorem patriam," is Latin for "They desire a better country."

Canadian winners of the Nobel Prize

Frederick Banting
for discovering insulin, in 1923
Lester B. Pearson
Prime Minister 1963-68, for peace in 1957
Gerhard Herzberg
for chemistry in 1971
Henny Taube
for chemistry in 1983
John Polanyi
for chemistry in 1986
Michael Smith
for chemistry in 1993
Bertram Brockhouse
for physics in 1994

There are many other awards that Canadians have received. One of the most prestigious is the Nobel Prize. Alfred B. Nobel was a Swedish scientist and inventor who left most of his vast fortune in trust to be awarded to individuals who had "confirmed the greatest benefit on mankind" in the fields of physics, chemistry, medicine, literature, and peace. Several Canadians have won the Nobel prize over the years.

During the opening ceremonies of the Olympic Games, the teams from each country parade into the stadium. Both the flag and a sign bearing the name of the country are proudly carried by members of each team.

The Olympic Games and the Commonwealth Games provide other opportunities for recognition. At the Olympics, athletes compete to be the best in the world at their sport. Many Canadians have won bronze, silver, and gold medals in both the summer and winter Olympic Games. The Commonwealth Games allow Canadian athletes to compete with athletes from other Commonwealth countries.

36

In the Canadian Armed Forces, the highest honour is the Victoria Cross. It recognizes soldiers for bravery and devotion to their country. Alexander Dunn, the first Canadian to win the Victoria Cross, won it while fighting for the British in the Crimean War of 1854-56. Other winners include:

- Billy Bishop, the air ace who is credited with shooting down seventy-two enemy planes during World War I.
- William Hall, from Nova Scotia, who won his VC in 1857 with the Royal Navy in India.
- John Osborn sacrificed his life to save the lives of his comrades at the Battle of Hong Kong, 1941, by falling on a grenade seconds before it exploded.

Special awards are not the only way to show appreciation for individual effort and achievement. Many people who contribute to a better life never receive awards. They do what they do out of a need for personal achievement or a desire to help their community. It is up to every one of us to applaud these individuals when we see them. They are the unsung heroes of Canada.

PROFILE

Elvis Stojko

Elvis Stojko is a unique individual in the world of competitive figure skating. A world champion and Olympic medalist, he has been skating since he was five years old. He showed his determination to succeed from an early age, and is known within the skating community to be a very hard worker.

Elvis is the third child born to two Canadian immigrants, Steve and Irene Stojko. Elvis's father came to Canada from Slovenia, and his mother came from Hungary, both in 1956. In Canada they met and married. Elvis's mother still sews all of his costumes by hand from patterns she designs herself.

Elvis has a very individual style. He uses his martial arts training in his skating, and has even used music from *Dragon: The Bruce Lee Story* in his programs. He skates in a very powerful, non-traditional way.

Success did not come easily to Elvis, who was always shy, and was teased in school because of his small size and unusual name. Even with all his success, he still has difficulty being the centre of attention. Elvis built up his confidence by studying psychology and philosophy, studies that helped him to improve his skating technique and overcome serious injuries. All of his hard work and determination have certainly paid off!

Questions ❓❓

1. Canada has had many Olympic medal winners, such as Myriam Bedard, Michael Smith, and Silken Laumann. Find out more about the life of one of these athletes.

Chapter Review 2

What We Have Learned

One of the main goals of multiculturalism is to respect the differences between individuals and to treat everyone fairly and equally. Every individual contributes to Canadian society. The rights of Canadian citizens are protected by the Canadian Charter of Rights and Freedoms. Tolerance and understanding are important for eliminating discrimination, prejudice, stereotyping, and racism from Canadian society. It is important to celebrate and value individual accomplishments.

Talk About

The grade 9 students at Springbank Community High School in Springbank, Alberta, chose to attend Steven Spielberg's Academy Award-winning movie, *Schindler's List,* on the International Day for the Elimination of Racial Discrimination. What is the connection? What might your class do to mark the same occasion?

Questions

1. What government document protects the rights and freedoms of Canadians?
2. How would you define racism?
3. What is the difference between a prejudice and a stereotype?
4. How does multiculturalism influence your life at school and at home? Do you think it is the same for other Canadians?

Activities

1. Sometimes people focus too much on their differences rather than their similarities. It is often surprising to find out how much we have in common with others. Once we begin to find common ground, we move towards a greater understanding of one another. Try this activity: Draw a large circle on a piece of paper and fill in all the things you can think of that make up who you are.

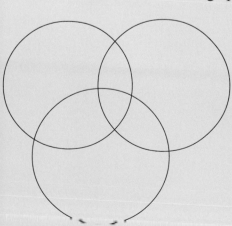

plays baseball
likes to skate
smiles a lot
loves pizza
goes sailing
favourite pets are
Dad is a pilot
dogs and cats
loves ice cream
good student
all family lives in Canada
brown hair   Mom works
has a goldfish

Together with two others in your class, draw three circles on a large piece of paper. Where the circles overlap, write the phrases you have in common with others. You can add phrases as you go even if they were not on your original circles. Are you surprised by the number of things you have in common?

Challenges

1. Write a personal statement about your behaviour towards others. How do you treat other people?

2. Have you ever remained silent when you should have spoken up? Take the opportunity now to write about what you should have said or done.

Skill Builders

1. Make a scrapbook of newspaper articles dealing with rights and freedoms. Compare the articles about Canada with the articles about other parts of the world. Are the same rights and freedoms at issue?

2. Develop your artistic skills by making a poster to illustrate one of the following ideas: prejudice, discrimination, stereotyping, or racism.

3. Become a journalist. Write an editorial for your local newspaper arguing in support of your position on multiculturalism.

Multiculturalism and the Community

Mini Table of Contents

3 Early Communities

I n order to understand the kind of country Canada is today, it is necessary to look back in time and examine its early communities. In the early days, people depended greatly upon one another. The community was very important, sometimes more important than the individual. Community **values** included family, education, marriage, work, and religion. These were the traditions and the beliefs that early Canadians valued above all others, because the survival of their communities depended upon them.

It is said that Canada has two "founding peoples": the French and the British. Over the years, these communities mixed and exchanged ideas, and often learned from one another, but still kept their separate identities.

Long before the arrival of the French and the British to what is now Canada, the land was occupied by many different Native groups. Some lived on the Plains and hunted buffalo. Others lived on the seacoast and relied mainly on fish for their survival. Others lived in the forest where they hunted moose and deer. The French and British colonists founded Canada in the midst of these Native groups.

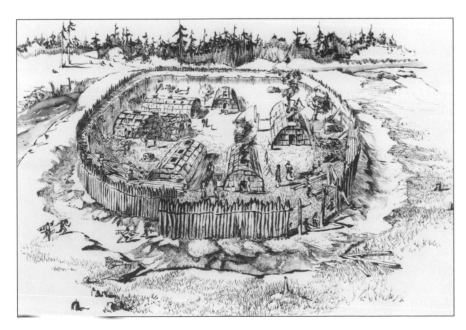

The earliest communities in what is now Canada consisted of many different Native groups. Altogether, there were more than fifty different cultural groups of Aboriginal Peoples, each with their own language and traditions.

Key Term

Values are beliefs and ways of doing things that are considered important, either by an individual or by an entire culture.

Life in early Canada was hard. It was also very different from what many newcomers had been used to in Europe. This image shows a missionary on a dog sled approaching a mission on the Mackenzie River.

When the first European colonists, the French, began arriving in the early 1600s, Native Peoples found themselves dealing with an unfamiliar culture. French ideas, behaviours, clothing, language, and way of life were very different from those in the Native communities. At first the two groups had difficulty understanding each other. After all, they did not speak the same language and their customs were very different. Each group tended to judge the other by its own standards. Naturally enough, each thought their way was best.

The two groups quickly got to know one another, however. The Native Peoples welcomed the newcomers to their land. They showed them the best places to hunt and fish and how to survive the cold Canadian winter. The French wished to obtain the valuable furs the Native Peoples possessed. For their part, the Native Peoples were eager to trade for the metal goods and blankets offered by the Europeans. Slowly, the two groups learned to live together.

Along with the fur traders, explorers, and settlers, the French sent missionaries to Canada to convert the Native Peoples to Christianity. Many of the early missionaries left detailed accounts of their impressions of the new land and its people. The extracts on the following pages are taken from their reports. They reveal the different opinions the French and the Native Peoples had about each other. As you read them, try to think about the values each group used to judge the other.

A French Viewpoint

The first example is from a report written in 1635 by Jean de Brébeuf, a Jesuit missionary who lived among the Hurons.

We see shining among them some rather noble moral virtues. You note, in the first place, a great love and union, which they are careful to cultivate by means of their marriages, of their presents, of their feasts, and of their frequent visits. On returning from their fishing, their hunting, and their trading, they exchange many gifts; if they have thus obtained something unusually good, even if they have bought it, or it has been given to them, they make a feast to the whole village with it. Their hospitality towards all sorts of strangers is remarkable; they present to them in their feasts the best of what they have prepared, and, as I have already said, I do not know if anything similar in this regard is to be found anywhere. They never close the door upon a stranger, and, once having received him into their houses, they share with him the best they have; they never send him away, and when he goes away of his own accord, he repays them by a simple "thank you."

If you were invited to view this ceremony, what would be your first impressions? Would you feel differently once you understood the meaning of the ceremony? How fair is it to judge the traditions of a particular culture before you fully understand them?

Think About

Do you think that one cultural group can speak accurately for another? Why or why not? Do you think that the Huron People might have described themselves differently? In what way?

A Native Person's Viewpoint

This is a story told by a Blackfoot man about his first glimpse of a European.

We (the Blackfoot) looked through the underbrush, and saw what we at first thought were bears, and afterward took to be persons, lifting logs and putting them up in a large pile. We crept closer, to where we could see better, and then concluded that these were not people. They were very woolly on the face. Long masses of hair hung down from their chins. They were not clothed—wore no robes.

When we got back to our camp, we told what we had seen; that to the south we had found animals that were very much like people—water animals. We said that these animals were naked. That some of them had red bodies, (wore red shirts) and some were black all over, except a red mark around the bodies and a fine red tail (the sash worn by the Hudson's Bay Men). Moreover, these people wore no robes or leggings and no breechcloths.

This description caused a great excitement in the camp. Some thought that the strange beings were water animals, and others that they were a new people. All the men of the camp started south to see what this could be. Before they left the camp, the head man told them to be very careful in dealing with the animals, not to interfere with them nor to get in their way, and try not to hurt them nor to anger them.

What do you think the Native Peoples thought when they saw strangers like this coureur du bois for the first time?

44

A Missionary's Viewpoint

This account is from a report by the missionary Gabriel Sagard. He is describing how he thought some Native Peoples viewed the French.

They called the French Agnonha in their language; that is, iron people. The Canadians (the Native Peoples around Québec city) and the Montagnais surname us Mistigoche, which in their language means wooden canoe or boat; they call us so because our ships and boats are made of wood and not bark as theirs are.

Since they reckoned that the greatest captains in France were endowed with the greatest mind, and possessing so great a mind they alone could make the most complicated things, such as axes, knives, kettles, etc., they concluded therefore that the King . . . made the largest kettles. . . .

They have such a horror of a beard that sometimes when they try to insult us they call us . . . Bearded, You have a beard. Moreover, they think it makes people more ugly and weakens their intelligence.

They think we have little intelligence in comparison to themselves.

These two drawings of Native Peoples were made by Europeans. What do you think the artists were trying to say about Native Peoples? In what ways do you think the drawings are inaccurate? Why do you think they are so different?

How Did Native Communities Change?

During the first 150 years of European settlement, the fur trade was the most important industry in Canada. To obtain the furs, the Europeans relied on the Native Peoples, who adapted their way of life so they could take part in this new business and obtain the trade goods that only the Europeans could provide.

The most destructive change brought by the fur trade was disease. The Europeans brought sicknesses like smallpox, measles, and tuberculosis to North America. These diseases were unknown in the New World, and the Native Peoples had no immunity. Epidemics swept through their villages, often wiping out entire populations.

The Beothuk People are a tragic example of the worst that could happen when Native Peoples and Europeans came into contact. The Beothuk lived in Newfoundland where they hunted wild game and fished in the rivers and lakes. The Europeans who came to Newfoundland built fishing stations on the shore, but they seldom stayed for the winter. While they were away, the Beothuk saw no harm in helping themselves to what the Europeans left behind. It was part of the Beothuk culture to share possessions. The fishermen, however, called it theft and often fired on the Beothuk for "stealing" their equipment.

As time passed, more and more Europeans began living on the island all year. They moved inland onto Beothuk hunting territory, and the two groups came into competition for animals and furs. The Beothuk had nowhere else to go, and eventually they died out, the victims of starvation and murder. Although there are some Aboriginal Peoples living in Newfoundland today, none are descendants of the Beothuk who originally lived there.

This is a painting titled "Three Indian Chiefs." Find evidence in the painting of how Europeans influenced the Aboriginal People.

A Culture Disappears

Shanawdithit was about twenty-four years old in 1823 when she was captured with her mother and sister by a party of settlers. After her family members died, Shanawdithit became the last surviving Beothuk. She was taken into the home of John Peyton in St. John's, and was given the name Nancy. She helped the Peyton family with their household chores, but was free to come and go as she pleased.

She seemed happy most of the time, but sometimes became gloomy, and would go off to the woods for days at a time.

A clergyman who met her described her as follows: *Her complexion was swarthy; her features were handsome; she was a tall figure and stood nearly six feet. When I showed her my watch, she put it to her ear and was amused with its tick. When a black lead pencil was put into her hand and a piece of white paper laid on the table, she was in raptures. She made a few marks on the paper to try the pencil; then, in one flourish she drew a deer perfectly, and what is more surprising, she began at the tip of the tail.*

Shanawdithit was also good at carving. She carved combs out of caribou horn, decorating them with elaborate patterns.

She was often visited by the merchant/explorer William Epps Cormack, who was eager to learn all he could about the Beothuks. He had crossed Newfoundland on foot, hoping to contact any of the surviving Beothuks. Shanawdithit had been learning some English and her knowledge of the language greatly improved with Cormack's help. In return, she taught him some of the Beothuk language. She told him about her tribe, its history and customs, and she drew pictures to illustrate what she was describing. Most of what we know today about the Beothuks is based on these drawings, and on the notes that Cormack made about his talks with Shanawdithit.

The Beothuks wore their hair long and plaited at the back of the head. In their hair, they stuck feathers, one of them usually straight up. They wore moccasins made of caribou skin in the winter, and went barefoot in the summer. During the winter they lived in wigwams, which were usually rectangular, but sometimes circular in shape. Nearby were their storehouses and places to smoke meat. They had large canoes, which they made from caribou skins and birch. Their deadliest weapon was the bow and arrow.

In 1829, Shanawdithit died of tuberculosis. She was only about twenty-nine years old. Today her drawings are in the Newfoundland Museum. They are a small reminder of a culture that once existed.

Questions

1. Imagine that you are the last surviving member of your culture. What drawings would you make to explain your culture to an outsider?
2. Research the Beothuk culture. Why was Shanawdithit the last surviving member?

Signing Treaties

Contact between Europeans and Native Peoples brought changes to both cultures. Europeans adopted the Aboriginal ways of travel, using snowshoes, toboggans, and bark canoes to go far into the interior of the country. They also adopted many foods and medicines that were unknown in Europe at the time.

Contact with Europeans changed the way of life of Native Peoples more dramatically. Missionaries tried to change the religious beliefs of the Native Peoples. Settlers wanted to occupy their land, and governments relocated them to small reserves and forced them to give up their traditional hunting lifestyle.

In some cases, land taken from the Native Peoples and given to the Europeans was done through **treaties**. Treaties are written agreements by which the Native Peoples gave the Europeans their territories in return for cash payments, small reserves of land, and guarantees that they would be able to continue to hunt and fish. The treaties covered a huge area stretching from northern Ontario across the West to the Rocky Mountains.

This map shows the treaty areas between 1850 and 1984.

INDIAN TREATIES AND AGREEMENTS IN CANADA

1-11	Numbered Treaties
WA(I)CSA	Western Arctic (Inuvialuit) Claims Settlement Act
JBNQA	James Bay and Northern Québec Agreement
NEQA	Northeastern Québec Agreement
RS	Robinson-Superior Treaty
RH	Robinson-Huron Treaty
W	Williams Treaty
*****	Exempt by Royal Proclamation

0   250   500   750 Km

WA(I)CSA
1984

11
1921

8
1899

10
1906

5b
1908

JBNQA
1975
and
NEQA
1978

5a
1875

9
1905

6a
1876

7
1877

2
1871

4
1874

1
1871

3
1873

RS
1850

*1763

RH
1850

W
1923

N

Becoming a Minority

As more and more Europeans arrived, they spread across Native Peoples' hunting lands. Soon the Europeans were a majority in many parts of the country. The Native Peoples became a minority in their own homelands.

The Native Peoples and Europeans had very different ideas about what the treaties between their nations meant. The Native Peoples believed that land was owned by the community or nation, not by individuals. They believed the land belonged to all generations, past and future, and to the plants and animals as well. They thought the treaties were agreements to share with the newcomers. The government, on the other hand, saw the treaties as legal purchases. According to their view, the Native Peoples gave up all claims to the land when they signed.

The Native Peoples who signed treaties gave up vast amounts of land that they had occupied for centuries. In return, the government set aside reserves for them to live on. Native Peoples were expected to live on these small pieces of land and support themselves by ranching and farming. The government agreed to provide schools for the children, and a small amount of cash for every person who lived on the reserve. The *Indian Act* of 1876 guaranteed Native Peoples the right to hunt and fish on their former land, providing they did not interfere with settlers.

The government saw reserves as places where the Native Peoples would live until they learned the "proper and civilized" way of life, as one official put it at the time. He meant that the Native Peoples had to give up their old ways and learn to live like the farm settlers. The government felt that it knew what was best for the Native Peoples.

Today there are almost 2 300 reserves in Canada, of which only about 840 are inhabited. During the last twenty years or so, Canadian policies that affect Native communities have changed. Native Peoples are challenging the treaties signed by their ancestors, claiming that many of the treaties have not been honoured. In 1982, the new Canadian Constitution recognized the rights of the Métis, the Inuit, and Native Peoples, who are making progress toward taking control of their own affairs. Many Native groups are working toward the goal of **self-government**.

This photograph was taken at Fort Pitt in 1884. The great Cree leader, Big Bear, is on the far right. Native Peoples and Europeans had very different ideas about what the treaties between their nations meant. Describe some of the differences.

Key Term

The ***Indian Act*** is the law by which the federal government regulates Native People's affairs in Canada. The first *Indian Act* was passed in 1876, but it has been changed many times since then.

Self-government is a right claimed by Aboriginal Peoples to control their own education, legal, justice, and social systems.

Banning the Potlach

Sometimes people from one culture try to force another culture to change. The potlatch ban is an example of the way in which one culture attempted to change another.

The potlatch was an important ceremony among the Native Peoples of the Pacific Coast. It had many purposes:

- it determined rank among individuals and tribes.
- it was a way of sharing wealth with the weakest and poorest in the community.
- it was used to restore the dignity of a chief who had suffered an insult.
- it was a peaceful alternative to war among various Native groups.
- it was part of installing a new chief, raising a totem pole, celebrating a marriage, mourning the dead, and marking other special occasions.

Feasting, singing, and dancing were all part of the potlatch, but it was the gift-giving that offended settlers, missionaries and government agents. Often a potlatch lasted several days, during which time the host gave away great quantities of blankets, cloth, and other gifts. This brought the host great respect in the community. Later, when guests hosted their own potlatches, they also were generous with their gifts.

The Europeans did not understand the nature of the ceremony and the importance of the potlatch to the Native Peoples. They saw it as a huge squandering of wealth that offended their own values of thrift. They pressed for a ban on the potlatch. On April 19, 1884, the federal government changed the *Indian Act* to read:

> *Every Indian or other person who engages in or assists in celebrating the Indian festival known as the "Potlatch" or in the Indian dance known as the "Tamanawas" is guilty of a misdemeanor, and shall be liable to imprisonment for a term of not more than six nor less than two months;... and any Indian or other person who encourages, either directly or indirectly, an Indian or Indians to get up such a festival or dance, or to celebrate the same, or who shall assist in the celebration of the same is guilty of a like offence and shall be liable to the same punishment.*

The Potlatch Law, as it came to be called, remained in force until 1951.

Making Choices

Discuss whether one culture should have the power and authority to impose change upon another.

A New Community is Born

From the earliest days of the fur trade, both French and British traders married Native women. Trading was far easier when traders were related by marriage to local Native communities. The children of French/Native marriages were called Métis; however, the children of the British/Native marriages had no formal name. Some people considered them Métis, while others called them "the country born."

Most Métis lived on the prairies in the region of the Red River Settlement in what is now southern Manitoba. When the fur traders retired, they often chose to settle along the Red River rather than take their families to an unfamiliar community.

Even so, many Métis were brought up in both cultures. Some fathers sent their sons to eastern Canada, or even to Europe, for their schooling. Other children were taught in Red River by Roman Catholic priests and nuns. Most Métis were French-speaking Catholics.

The Métis were equally influenced by aspects of Native Peoples' cultures such as hunting and trapping techniques. Although some Métis were farmers, and others worked as packers for the Hudson's Bay Company, many made their living hunting buffalo. The Métis were masters in the art of "running" the buffalo—riding fearlessly among the animals to shoot them down as they thundered in panic across the plains.

The buffalo hunt was the focus of Métis life. Two large hunts occurred each year. They were highly-organized affairs with elected leaders and captains. Special rules governed the hunt, with severe penalties for anyone who disobeyed. The hunt could not begin until the leader gave the signal. Nobody could claim a buffalo that another hunter killed. The rules were intended to ensure fairness and order during the hunt, which was a very dangerous activity. The principles governing the buffalo hunt also applied to other community matters.

Because they had their own laws and customs, the Métis felt that they were a separate culture with their own unique identity. They did not totally identify with either European or Native Peoples. The Métis saw themselves as a new people.

Although the Métis were children of French/Native marriages, they did not really identify with either culture. Instead, they thought of themselves as a separate culture with their own traditions and laws.

Think About

What factors might cause a person of more than one ethnic heritage to choose to adopt the culture of one of his or her parents instead of the other?

51

The Métis Struggle for Community

Like other Aboriginal Peoples, the Métis of Western Canada felt threatened by the arrival of settlers. Most of them had lived in the Red River area for generations, but they had no official title to their land, no piece of paper to prove that they owned it. In 1869, they were concerned when government surveyors arrived to measure out lots for new settlers. The surveying was done so that the Canadian government could buy the whole area from the Hudson's Bay Company.

Most Métis lived in the vicinity of the Red River Colony in what is now Manitoba. How did settlement by Europeans threaten the Métis culture and lifestyle?

The Métis believed that their way of life, based largely on the buffalo hunt, was at risk. They knew that the arrival of more farm settlers would mean the end of the buffalo. Moreover, most of the new settlers were English-speaking Protestants from Ontario, whereas most Métis were French-speaking Catholics. The Métis worried that the settlers might become a majority in Red River. Not only were Métis lands threatened, but also their culture and religion.

Led by Louis Riel, the Métis organized themselves to protect their rights and decided to resist the new regime. This movement has been called "the Red River Resistance" of 1869-70. The Métis set up a temporary government to establish orderly rule, and drew up a **List of Rights** that they sent to the Canadian government in Ottawa.

The List of Rights asked that the Red River area be made into a province. It asked that Métis land, French language rights, and the Roman Catholic religion all be protected. The Canadian government agreed to many of these terms, and in 1870, a new province, Manitoba, was created. Eventually both French and English were made official languages, and Catholics and Protestants received separate school systems.

Riel was a hero to the Métis, but the Canadian government considered him a rebel. When Prime Minister John A. Macdonald sent troops to Red River to prevent further trouble, Riel fled to the United States.

Key Term

The **List of Rights** is a list of demands the provisional Métis Government presented to the Federal Government in 1869.

During the years that followed, large numbers of Métis left Manitoba, moving west and north onto the plains where they formed communities and continued to live as farmers and buffalo hunters. However, this way of life did not last for long. By the late 1870s, the great herds of buffalo had been killed off to supply the American and Canadian market for hides.

The near disappearance of the buffalo affected all the people of the prairies. Native Peoples, faced with starvation, moved to reserves where they had land, schools, and medical and economic assistance provided for them by a treaty with the Canadian government. The Métis had no reserves. Many of them had small farms in the Saskatchewan River country, but they did not have title to this land, and they soon faced the same problems they had at Red River. Settlers continued to move west, and once again threatened to take over Métis lands.

In 1885, the Métis turned to Louis Riel for help. Once again he became their leader and spokesperson. He asked the government to settle their land claims, but the government took no action. Métis discontent escalated into armed conflict. The government sent a well-equipped army to the West, and the Northwest Resistance of 1885 was soon over. The Métis were defeated and Louis Riel was sentenced to death for treason. He was hanged in Regina, Saskatchewan, on November 6, 1885.

Louis Riel was the leader of the Métis people in their struggles with the Canadian government. He and the Métis council drew up a List of Rights. How did this list, and the events which followed, change the Métis community?

Making Choices ✓

How should the Canadian government have treated the Métis land claims? If the claims had been treated differently, do you think the Northwest Resistance of 1885 would have occurred? Explain your answer.

Keeping Traditions Alive

From the arrival of the first settlers to the Northwest Resistance of 1885, the Native Peoples of the prairies underwent many changes. Both Native Peoples and the Métis were now minorities in the land they had once considered their own. Where they had previously looked after their needs, they were now dependent upon government rations for their survival.

The Métis, as a culture caught between two cultures, lost a great deal with these changes. Unlike many Native Peoples, the Métis had no reserves on which they could live together and share their traditions. Some Métis lived in fairly large communities like St-Paul-des-Métis in Alberta, but most were left to adapt to a changing environment on their own. Although many government agents and missionaries assumed that the Aboriginal Peoples would be readily **assimilated** into the majority culture, Aboriginal Peoples such as the Métis have kept their cultural traditions alive. Even though the Métis lost much, they achieved something very important. They gained a national hero—Louis Riel—and a proud history of survival.

The Métis could adapt more easily to the changes occurring around them; they were already part of the European culture. It was harder for the Native Peoples, who found themselves in a difficult situation. While the reserves helped to keep their cultures alive, reserves also kept them apart from the new Canadian culture.

Because of the differences in their origins, traditions, and lifestyles, the Aboriginal Peoples and the European settlers often misunderstood one another. These misunderstandings often led to discrimination against the Aboriginal Peoples.

Assimilation is what happens when one cultural group absorbs the characteristics of another. In the case of the Aboriginal Peoples, the government tried to force them to assimilate. Sometimes assimilation can happen naturally and voluntarily.

The Métis adapted to the European culture with more success than many Native groups. They quickly became experienced blacksmiths, saddlers, and wheelwrights.

The French and British

So far we have viewed European culture as a single force. In reality, each European nation had its own culture, just as each group of Native Peoples, the Métis, and the Inuit had their own cultures. For the first 150 years of settlement, two European cultures clashed in North America—the French and the British.

Both France and Britain created their first North American settlements in the early 1600s. The French settled in Nova Scotia and along the St. Lawrence River in what is now Québec. They established the first colony in Canada, Port Royal, near the Bay of Fundy. A few years later, they built a tiny settlement on the St. Lawrence River. This colony depended on the rich fur trade for its survival. Towns such as Québec, Montréal, and Trois-Rivières were founded along the river. Gradually the French explored inland and eventually claimed large areas of present-day Canada, as well as much of the interior of the present-day United States.

Meanwhile, the British settled along the eastern seacoast of North America, south of the French. British settlers began building colonies, the first of which was Jamestown, Virginia, in 1607. Other colonies began at Plymouth and Boston. These were the beginnings of the thirteen New England colonies, which eventually became the United States. The British also established colonies in Newfoundland and on Hudson Bay, where they claimed ownership of a vast part of the west and the north, a territory they called Rupert's Land. However, much of Rupert's Land was also claimed by France, as was Newfoundland.

The British and the French were already long-standing rivals in Europe where they had fought each other for centuries. In North America, they found a new cause for conflict. Both nations wanted to control the profitable fur trade. By 1760, after years of warfare, the British finally defeated the French armies in New France. Almost all of eastern North America then came under British control.

Towns like Québec were built along the St. Lawrence River. Samuel de Champlain, explorer, mapmaker, and founder of Québec, sketched this drawing of the early settlement.

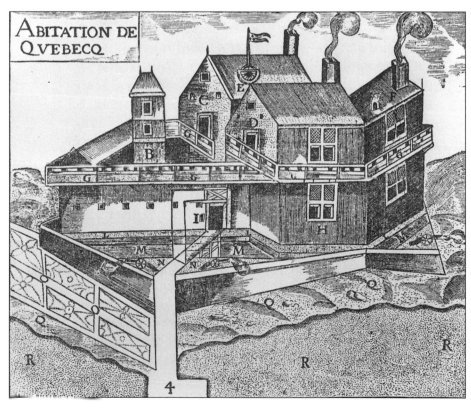

55

With their victory, the British took responsibility for a population of about 60 000 French-speaking colonists. They allowed the French colonists in Québec to retain their language, religion, and other traditions. They felt safe in doing so because they expected that English-speaking Protestants would soon become the majority. However, the French had developed a strong sense of their own culture over the years. They considered themselves Canadiens and were determined to resist any attempts to make them British.

In 1867, the different colonies of what was called British North America came together to create the Dominion of Canada. In the new Dominion, power was divided between a federal government and several provinces. Both English and French were the official languages of the federal government and its courts. Each province controlled its own education system. These arrangements made it possible for French-speaking Quebeckers, or Québécois, to preserve their language and culture in a country where the majority of people spoke English.

Today, French is the everyday language in the province of Québec. The French culture is flourishing there. The Québécois create poetry, plays, novels, music, and art that reflect their culture. Their determination to keep their culture alive has been an important factor shaping the history of Canada.

PROFILE

British Settlers in North America

The first British colony in North America was built in 1607 in Virginia. It was called Jamestown, after King James I of England. The British colonists faced a harsh climate and conditions that made life difficult for survival. A captain by the name of John Smith helped the settlers in Jamestown by learning from the Native Peoples. He taught the settlers how to grow tobacco, which became a very valuable crop for the colony.

In 1621, King James I granted Sir William Alexander the right to establish a new colony. It was called Nova Scotia. However, Nova Scotia was already settled by the French, who called it Acadia. The French and British fought over this area for many years until finally the British were victorious in 1760. British settlers moved up from New England to occupy the land, and Nova Scotia became a self-governing colony. More people were needed to settle the land, so advertisements were sent to Scotland asking for settlers. Many farmers and fishermen decided to come to Nova Scotia, and during the late 1700s, about 25 000 people left Scotland for North America. This Scottish heritage is still evident in the unique culture of Nova Scotia today.

How have the French and English co-existed in Canada over the years?

The British guaranteed the French certain rights. Why should we be so surprised that they are exercising their rights? The British allowed them to keep their own identity.

Why should we all be forced to speak French when we do not need it in all parts of the country?

There has been little give-and-take over the centuries. The French and the English still do not see eye-to-eye on many things. Quebeckers still want to have their own country.

It's nice to live in a bilingual and bicultural country. We have learned a great deal from one another. Canadians are a combination of both French and British history and culture. That's what we are. We can't change history.

Both the French and English have a lot in common. We are all Canadians. We both have the same history, and we share the same values, laws, and political systems.

Making Choices

The relationship between the French and English in Canada has gone through many changes over the years. These viewpoints express different opinions about that relationship. What is your own viewpoint about the way in which the French and English have learned to live together in Canada?

57

What We Have Learned

Canada is a community of communities. It has been built by many communities, including the Aboriginal Peoples and the groups that came later from other countries. As cultures and communities came together, changes occurred. Sometimes new communities were formed, such as the Métis. The early communities of French, British, and Native Peoples laid the foundations of modern Canada.

Talk About

1. Who are Canada's two "founding peoples"?
2. Explain the origins of the Métis people.
3. Describe a culture that ceased to exist in Canada, and explain what happened to it.
4. Explain what may happen when cultures come into contact. Give specific examples.
5. What is a treaty?
6. What rights did the British guarantee the French colonists in Canada?
7. What has been the result of the British decision to allow the French colonists to keep their religion and language?

Questions

Discuss assumptions that have been made about French, British, and Aboriginal Peoples throughout history. Looking back, do you think these assumptions were correct?

Activities

1. Clip newspaper and magazine articles that illustrate ways in which particular cultures are changing. Collect these articles in a scrapbook and prepare a summary.
2. In web form, summarize what you know about early communities in Canada.
3. Create a collage of elements you consider part of your culture. Compare collages with your classmates. Are they similiar?

Challenges

1. Create your own definition of "founding peoples."
2. In small groups, prepare a list of values important to your classmates, your school, and your community. Compare your group's list with others.
3. With your classmates, create a time capsule to be opened in one hundred years. Include a list of events, people, and things that are most important to you. Explain the signficance of the items on your list to your classmates. What did you learn about yourself? Your class?

Skill Builders

1. Throughout history, many groups have developed "lists of rights" that spell out their beliefs and causes. Do some research to find a group other than the Métis who have also put forward a list to try to bring about change. What features and goals do the Métis list and the list you found have in common?

List of Rights set out by the Métis:

- ❑ That the people have the right to elect their own Legislature.
- ❑ That the Legislature has the power to pass all laws local to the Territory over the veto of the Executive by a two-thirds vote.
- ❑ That no act of the Dominion Parliament (local to the Territory) be binding on the people until sanctioned by the Legislature of the Territory.
- ❑ That all Sheriffs, Magistrates, Constables, School Commissioners, etc., be elected by the people.
- ❑ A free Homestead and pre-emption Land Law.
- ❑ That a portion of the public lands be appropriated to the benefit of Schools, the building of Bridges, Roads and Public Buildings.
- ❑ That it be guaranteed to connect Winnipeg by Rail with the nearest line of Railroad, within a term of five years; the land grant to be subject to the Local Legislature.
- ❑ That for the term of four years all Military, Civil, and Municipal expenses be paid out of the Dominon funds.
- ❑ That the Military be composed of the inhabitants now existing in the Territory.
- ❑ That the English and French languages be common in the Legislature and Courts, and that all Public Documents and Acts of the Legislature be published in both languages.
- ❑ That the judge of the Supreme Court speak the English and French languages.
- ❑ That treaties be concluded and ratified between the Dominion Government and the several tribes of Indians in the Territory to ensure peace on the frontier.
- ❑ That we have a fair and full representation in the Canadian Parliament.
- ❑ That all privileges, customs and usages existing at the time of the transfer be respected.

−1869

59

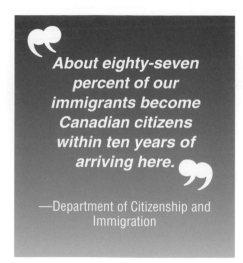
Key Term

Mainstream culture comprises the values and traditions of the majority.

Think About

Reflect on the different circumstances that immigrants to Canada may have left behind in their home countries.

4 Building Communities Through Immigration

Three groups have played an important role in Canada's development. Each of these three groups has had an influence on our communities. These groups are the Native Peoples, the early British and French settlers, and the immigrants. As we saw in the previous chapter, the first colonists to come to Canada were the French and the British. They both interacted with the Native Peoples who were already living here. Over time, immigrants from other countries began to arrive, first in small numbers, then in great waves of newcomers.

In 1871, Canada's population was 3.6 million people. Today the population is more than twenty-five million people, of which a large proportion are immigrants. Immigrants have played, and will continue to play, an important role in the growth and development of Canada. They come to this country full of hopes, dreams, and desires for a better life. Many leave difficult situations in their own countries. Some even leave their families, hoping to be reunited once they are established here in Canada. Many immigrants come to Canada with talents and skills that help to build the country and make it prosperous.

Canada has developed immigration policies to accommodate the newcomers. Because there are always more immigration applicants than Canada can accept, decisions must be made about who should be allowed to enter and who should not. These decisions are usually based on the values, attitudes, and needs of the people who are already living here.

When immigrants come to Canada, they must adjust to living in a new country with a different culture. Over time, they may give up parts of their own culture and become more like the majority, or **mainstream culture**. This process, known as assimilation, is slow and occurs in a number of different stages. New immigrants do not

60

It takes time for a newcomer to become familiar with Canadian customs, values, clothing styles, language, and even the weather.

usually adopt Canadian customs right away. First they have to learn what norms, values, language, dress, and lifestyles people in their new community accept. Then they begin to get involved in local activities. They may go to school, or start a business, or join a club, and gradually they begin to speak and act like members of the mainstream. In many cases, personal contact and involvement with others helps to break down the stereotypes that individuals from different backgrounds have about each other. At the same time, the newcomers may retain some of the traditions, special holidays, and even the language of their original country.

Assimilation may go as far as the complete acceptance of the mainstream culture. Newcomers sometimes choose to intermarry and stop practising the traditions of their original heritage. They begin to think of themselves as part of the mainstream culture, rather than as a separate group. In this case, complete assimilation has occurred.

In other cases, immigrant groups choose to remain separate, or **segregated**, from the mainstream. Sometimes it is the mainstream culture that does not want or allow the newcomers to participate fully. In extreme cases of segregation, rules and laws are made to keep people separate. Canadian laws and institutions have generally welcomed newcomers, and tried to ease their transition to life in Canada.

Segregated means being separate or apart.

61

Hutterite Communities

Sometimes groups choose to live apart from the rest of society. Hutterites, Mennonites, and Doukhobors are examples of groups that most often choose to be segregated. Read about how people in a Hutterite community choose to live, and how that community relates to the mainstream society.

The Hutterites are a religious group that was persecuted for its beliefs in its original homeland in Eastern Europe. They came to live in Canada in search of the freedom to practise their unique way of life. Hutterites live in small farming colonies, each consisting of several families. The members of the colony own everything in common. They share their land, buildings, machinery, and money. The only things they own individually are clothes and a few personal possessions.

Hutterites work together for the common good, and have been very successful farmers. As each colony reaches a certain size, it subdivides, buys new land, and begins a new colony. Hutterite colonies in Western Canada have been growing in size and number. For the most part, Hutterites avoid contact with the wider society. They wear old-fashioned clothing, they do not vote or run for political office, they speak a German dialect, and they have their own schools. Rarely do they allow radios, television, newspapers, or photographs in their communities.

Some people feel that as the Hutterite colonies continue to grow, there will be less land for

Working together for the common good of the colony is an important Hutterite value. How does this differ from mainstream Canadian culture?

non-Hutterites. Since the Hutterite colonies are self-sufficient, merchants in the surrounding area fear that they will lose business. In January 1983, an organization of rural municipalities in southern Alberta approved a motion to discourage Hutterites from owning more than a certain amount of land in a single municipality. The Hutterites feel that this interferes with their right to practise their way of life.

Questions

1. What are some other groups similar to the Hutterites? List their contributions to Canada.
2. Why is it important that the Hutterites and other minority groups be free to live as they wish?
3. Do you agree with the 1983 motion to regulate how much land the Hutterites may own? Why or why not?

A Short History of Immigration to Canada

The story of immigration to Canada goes back many years, to the first French colonists struggling to make a life for themselves on the shores of the St. Lawrence River and the Bay of Fundy. It is a story that contains some elements of which we are not so proud; however, it is also a story full of moments that make us very proud. Since Canada will always need immigrants to expand its population, it is also a story that will never end.

In the early years before Confederation in 1867, the people who came to Canada were mainly from Europe, the British Isles, and the United States. There were no policies that stopped people from choosing Canada as their home. French and British rulers saw settlers as a means to develop the resources of the colonies. Still, Canada was isolated and had a forbidding climate, so it was not always attractive to people seeking a new life. Settlement grew slowly and with great difficulty in the early years.

This advertisement encouraged people to come live in Canada. Why would people want to leave their home in favour of a free farm in Canada?

Think About

What would it have been like to settle in early Canada?

THE STORY OF IMMIGRATION

1605
Champlain establishes Port Royal in Acadia (Nova Scotia) and the Acadian community is founded.

1607
The first of the British colonies is built at Jamestown in Virginia.

1608
Champlain builds a habitation on the site of Québec City.

1663-73
Talon welcomes the "King's Daughters," 800 girls who were sent from France to be married in New France. This is the first instance of sponsored immigration to Canada.

1751
The first English Jewish people settle in Halifax.

1753
Germans settle at Lunenberg, Nova Scotia.

1758
5 000 to 6 000 New Englanders settle in Nova Scotia.

1763
Canada becomes a British colony. Disbanded British troops receive land grants.

THE LOYALIST LANDING PLACE
1784

On June 16, 1784, a party of some 250 United Empire Loyalists landed from bateaux near this site and established the first permanent white settlement in Adolphustown Township. They had sailed from New York in the fall of 1783 under the leadership of Major Peter Van Alstine (1747-1811), a Loyalist of Dutch ancestry, and passed the winter at Sorel. Van Alstine was later appointed a Justice of the peace, represented this area in the first Legislative Assembly of Upper Canada and built at Glenora the earliest grist-mill in Prince Edward County.

Erected by the Ontario Archaeological and Historic Sites Board.

Loyalists were among the earliest English-speaking settlers in Ontario.

During the American Revolution (1775-1783), many people who remained loyal to Britain came north to Canada. They did not want the American colonies to become independent. Their views made them unpopular in the United States, and they had to escape the persecution they suffered for supporting the British Crown. These people were known as **United Empire Loyalists**, and the British government rewarded their loyalty by providing them with supplies and land in Canada.

Most Loyalists were of British origin; others were Blacks and Native Peoples. All Loyalists felt a strong tie to Britain, and they established a strong British culture wherever they settled.

Many Loyalists came to the Maritime colonies, where they settled in Nova Scotia, or in the colony of New Brunswick, which was created especially for them. There is still a strong Loyalist element in the Maritime provinces, and several cities have Loyalist Days celebrations each year. Among the Nova Scotia Loyalists, many were Blacks, slaves who came with their owners, or former slaves who sought freedom from persecution in a new land. Some managed to make a home for themselves; others eventually left Nova Scotia and went to Africa.

Other Loyalists came to Upper Canada (now Ontario), which became a colony separate from Québec in 1791. Among this group was a small number of Mohawk families that settled on land along the Grand River. Their leader was Joseph Brant, after whom the city of Brantford, Ontario, is named.

During the 1800s, immigrants arrived in Canada from Ireland, Scotland, England, the United States, and Germany. Canada experienced a huge wave of immigration, especially during the period 1815-1850 when famine in Ireland and land shortages in Scotland forced tens of thousands of people to seek new lives overseas. In Canada, these

United Empire Loyalists were American colonists who stayed loyal to Britain during the American Revolution. Many thousands came north to live in Canada.

1771

John MacDonald and 200 followers begin the Scottish exodus to Canada. Eleven million people leave Britain for North America between 1770 and 1890.

1784

20 000 Loyalists arrive in Canada from the United States, including Germans, Scots, Mennonites, Quakers, Blacks, and Native Peoples.

1815

Lord Selkirk establishes a Scottish colony at Red River.

1818

The first Irish immigrants arrive. By 1826, there are 20 000 in the Lake Erie area.

These are Chinese labourers hired to build the Canadian Pacific Railway. Why was the building of a railway so important to the government?

immigrants opened up the backwoods areas for farming, took jobs in the lumber camps, or built canals and railways. It was a thriving time as the population grew rapidly and new towns and businesses boomed.

By Confederation, farm land was in short supply in eastern Canada. The government saw the need to open the West to settlers. A necessary first step was the construction of a railway across the West, the Canadian Pacific Railway. Thousands of Chinese people were hired to work on the railway. When it was finished in 1885, many of the Chinese stayed in Canada, sending for their families and settling mainly in British Columbia.

Life was hard for early settlers. Describe some of the difficulties faced by these settlers.

1819	1840–50	1840-61	1858
25 000 British arrive in a single year.	A period of intense German and Scandinavian migration due to poor crops, industrialization, and the consolidation of new farms.	Many Blacks come to Canada through the "Underground Railroad," the name given to the movement of Black slaves who were fleeing from the United States with the help of people in the north.	The first Chinese immigrants come via the United States to pan for gold.

1830-40

Germans from the United States and Europe settle in Waterloo County, Ontario.

The Potato Famine in Ireland

Read about how the Potato Famine in Ireland brought thousands of immigrants to Canada in the 1840s. Was the choice to leave home always the right one?

For centuries, the British held political control in Ireland. They tried to impose their own culture, including the Protestant religion, on the Irish People. Irish Catholics were the majority, but they had very few privileges. Most of the landlords were Protestants, and many were British.

By 1840, there were about eight million Irish, nearly all of whom were poor tenant farmers. Since the 1820s, some of the Protestants had been immigrating to Canada, attracted by offers of cheap land. Irish Catholics preferred to go to the United States where they would be free of British control. In the mid-1840s, the potato famine caused Catholics as well as Protestants to come to Canada in large numbers.

In Ireland, the main source of food was the potato. In 1845, a disease struck the potato crop, bringing famine to the countryside. The disease came again the next year, and again in the following years. The poorest Irish were in a desperate position. They had nothing to eat and no money for rent and taxes. The landlords turned them off the land. Meanwhile, many were dying of hunger. At least a million and a half Irish died of

This Irish colonist left Ireland during hard times and famine to find a better life in Canada.

starvation and disease between 1846 and 1852.

Many of the Irish decided to leave their homeland. More than a million left between 1846 and 1852. During these years, about 400 000 Irish entered Canada through the port of Québec alone. Since the majority of Irish were Catholics, so were the majority of Irish immigrants. These Irish Catholics harboured a deep hatred of the British, and many of them later went to live in the United States. Some Catholics remained, of course, but it was mostly Protestant Irish who settled permanently in Canada. By 1871, twenty-four percent of all Canadians were of Irish origin, making the Irish the second-largest ethnic minority after the French.

Into the Twentieth Century

The government decided to promote the development of the West by launching a campaign to attract immigrants who were interested in becoming farmers. Clifford Sifton, the Minister of the Interior, was largely responsible for bringing immigrants to the West. Sifton wanted to attract immigrants to Canada who would be able to farm the challenging landscape of the prairies. Many pamphlets and posters advertising Western Canada and promising free land to immigrants were sent to the United States, Britain, and Europe. This became known as Sifton's "open-door policy," and it attracted thousands of people from different countries.

The door was not open to everyone, however. Sifton did not welcome newcomers who wanted to settle in the cities. He thought that they would not be able to find jobs, or that they might take employment away from native-born Canadians. Nevertheless, many newcomers did settle in cities like Montréal, Toronto, Hamilton, Winnipeg, and Vancouver, where they contributed greatly to the economic prosperity of the country.

Many British Canadians protested Sifton's policies. They feared that so many immigrants from different countries would not be able to fit in with the Canadian way of life. There was an outcry against the settlers "in sheepskin coats" who seemed so different in their habits and often could not speak English.

Despite these fears, most of the immigrants eventually assimilated to the Canadian life. However, government policy was later tightened to restrict the entrance of some visible minority cultural

Boatloads of immigrants arrived in Canada in the early 1900s, carrying people who dreamed of a better, more prosperous life in a new land.

1865

Poles settle at Wilno in Ontario.

1872

Danes settle at New Denmark in New Brunswick.

1874

Mennonites settle near Winnipeg.

1875

The establishment of a colony of Icelanders at Gimli, Manitoba.

1881–84

15 700 Chinese come from Hong Kong and Canton to work on the railway.

1886–1888

Hungarians settle in Esterhazy, Saskatchewan.

1890–1900

300 000 Mormons, Hutterites, and other groups arrive in Canada.

1891–1911

75 000 Ukranian settlers arrive.

groups. In 1923, for example, Chinese immigration into Canada was halted, and until the policy changed in 1947, virtually no Chinese people were allowed to enter. Immigration from Japan was also stopped for several years. Officials made Black immigration almost impossible. Although no specific regulations refused Blacks admittance, officials ensured they were rejected for various "health" reasons. Blacks were warned that they should not waste time and money trying to get into Canada.

During the Great Depression of the 1930s, many Canadians lost their jobs. Because of the poor economy, officials tried to keep newcomers out of Canada rather than encouraging them to immigrate. In 1933, Adolf Hitler began his rule in Germany. Many people who opposed him, especially

Jewish people, wanted to leave Germany to escape persecution. Despite such circumstances, Canadian officials refused to allow Jewish people to enter the country.

Canada is a nation built by immigrants, but there have been episodes when groups have been kept out because of prejudice against them by the mainstream culture.

This second-hand store in Edmonton in 1918 is just one of many businesses started by newcomers to Canada.

1899

Dukhobors settle in the West.

1896–1914

Three million immigrants arrive, including Italians, Jewish people, Russians, Ukrainians, Germans, Scandinavians, and the British. It is one of the greatest population movements in world history.

1914

A group of 376 East Indians are refused admission to Canada at Vancouver.

1931–39

Only 147 000 immigrants arrive during these years.

1945–75

After World War II (1939–45), Canada takes in many refugees and people who were turned away from their countries—Jewish people, Poles, Czechs, Slovaks, Lithuanians, Latvians, Estonians, Ukranians, and others. Germans, Italians, Dutch, and British also enter the country. People come from many new areas as well: the West Indies, Greece, Portugal, the near East, the Far East, and Asia.

Changing Reasons for Immigration

In 1947, just after World War II, Prime Minister William Lyon Mackenzie King made a statement outlining Canada's new immigration policy. He announced that his government would allow the following people into the country:

- British subjects and citizens of the United States who met certain standards of health and character, and who showed that they were not likely to become burdens in Canada;
- relatives of Canadian citizens;
- people qualified to work in the primary industries that had shortages of workers;
- some **refugees, displaced persons** and Polish ex-soldiers.

This is what Prime Minister King said about Canadian immigration at the end of the war:

> *The population of Canada at present is about 12 000 000. By 1951, in the absence of immigration, it is estimated that our population would be less than 13 000 000, and that by 1971, without immigration, the population would be approximately 14 600 000. We cannot ignore the danger that lies in a small population attempting to hold so great a heritage as ours.*

King's policy differed from past policies in two ways.

First, he was willing to give special consideration to the relatives of Canadians, using immigration to bring families together. This became known as the sponsorship system. Families sponsored their relatives by agreeing to help them get settled once they arrived. Those who were sponsored had a better chance of getting into Canada than those who were not.

Second, refugees received special consideration. Refugees are people who seek a safe haven when their personal freedom or safety is at risk in their home country.

By the 1950s, Canada had removed many barriers to immigration. Economic reasons remained the strongest reasons for accepting immigrants. The country's booming economy needed skilled workers, and many of the people once listed as undesirable were now permitted to immigrate.

Sponsorship greatly increased immigration from European countries where cultures placed a lot of emphasis on the family. In both Italy and Greece, for example, people feel a great loyalty to their family. They expect that even distant relatives will help one another. During the 1950s, more than a quarter of a million immigrants came to Canada from Italy, many under the sponsorship program.

1955

Canada accepts some immigrants from the Caribbean as domestic workers.

1956–58

37 000 Hungarians come to Canada, fleeing an unsuccessful revolution in their homeland. Many British citizens, forced out of Egypt after the Suez Crisis, immigrate to Canada.

Think About

Would Prime Minister King's policy be accepted today? Why? Why not?

Key Term

A **refugee** is defined by the United Nations as "a person with a well-founded fear of persecution based on race, religion, nationality, social group, or political opinion."

Displaced persons are people left homeless in their own country as a result of war, famine, or a political disturbance.

Most settled in cities in Ontario. They took jobs in small business and industry, and many went into the construction industry.

During the post-war years, many immigrants also came from Britain. They often found it easy to fit in because they spoke English and shared many Canadian customs. Britain was going through hard times after the war. It had spent a lot of money on the war effort. Food was still rationed. People were allowed only a limited portion of meat or butter each week. By contrast, Canada was experiencing an era of prosperity. Britons saw the opportunity for a better life here.

In 1967, Canada's immigration policies changed again with the introduction of a point system. The government no longer gave preference to people because of their race or cultural background. Instead, new regulations defined four classes of immigrants: family, independent, business, and refugee. Applicants received points according to their age, education, occupation, the area where they wished to settle, their knowledge of French or English, and the demand for workers with their skills. Depending on which class they were in, applicants became eligible to become immigrants when they received a certain number of points. The whole idea of the point system was to obtain immigrants who could make the best contribution to Canadian society.

In 1986, the federal government relaxed immigration policies for successful business people. These potential immigrants could by-pass some of the hurdles faced by other applicants and qualify as "investors" if they had personal worth of at least $500 000 and promised to invest in Canada. In 1989, most of those applying in these business categories were from Hong Kong, Taiwan, Britain, and the United States. Critics say that this policy means that anyone can buy their way into Canada. The government estimated, however, that these immigrants would bring about thirty-three billion dollars to Canada, and create as many as 15 000 new jobs with their investments.

Canada has often been a safe haven for refugees. Since the 1950s, this country has taken in people escaping war and persecution in Hungary, Czechoslovakia, Chile, Somalia, and Vietnam, to name just a few places. In 1986, the United Nations honoured Canada for its generous policies toward refugees.

Special protection for refugees still exists through the Canadian Immigration and Refugee Board. Refugees must go through special hearings to prove that they are at risk in their home countries before they are accepted. In 1988, over 35 000 refugees came to Canada. Not all were allowed to stay. A new system was put in place in 1989 to screen out people who were making false applications.

Between 1950 and 1980, the origins of Canadian

1960–1970

American "draft dodgers" seek asylum in Canada.

1967

New regulations remove all restrictions regarding nationality and ethnic origin. In the selection of immigrants, the government places strong emphasis on education and job skills.

1967–74

The government looks mainly for highly skilled immigrants. Immigration greatly increases from Hong Kong, India, and the Caribbean.

1968–69

Russia invades Czechoslovakia. Canada accepts 12 000 Czechs who have fled their homeland.

1970

Canada accepts a small number of Tibetans after China invades Tibet.

1972

Canada accepts 7 000 people of South Asian origin who have been forced out of Uganda.

immigrants began to change. Most still came from Britain and the United States, but increasing numbers were coming from the Far East. By the 1980s, more immigrants came from places like Vietnam, India, and Hong Kong than from European countries. In 1990, Hong Kong ranked first as a source of new Canadian immigrants.

A Dutch family on their way to Canada in 1954. After World War II, many Dutch people came to Canada as part of a program sponsored by the government of The Netherlands, which paid all their travel expenses.

1973–74

Canada accepts several thousand refugees from Chile after the Chilean government falls to the military.

1974

Amnesty is proclaimed for all immigrants who entered Canada illegally.

1974–80

The government looks primarily for skilled workers. The range of countries from which immigrants come continues to expand.

1976

Several thousand Vietnamese refugees come to Canada after the Vietnam War.
The Immigration Act in use today is passed. It changes the way refugees are determined.

There were two main reasons for this change. One was that people no longer had such strong reasons to leave Europe. The economy there was much healthier than it had been after World War II, and people could make a good living in their own homelands. They did not think it was necessary to look for opportunities overseas. Even the less prosperous countries—Italy, Greece, and Portugal, for example—were far better off than than they had been at the end of the war.

The second reason was the implementation of Canada's point system of immigration. With this system, the government no longer gave preference to people from specific countries, but instead gave preference to people who met certain criteria, no matter where they came from. Since people from such countries as Italy, Greece, and Portugal did not always have the skills the government was looking for, immigration from these countries declined.

Over the years, the immigration process has changed many times. However, the main goals of Canadian policies have remained the same: to reunite families, to protect refugees, and to promote Canada's economic development.

Selecting Immigrants Today

Each year, many thousands of people apply to live permanently in Canada. In order to deal fairly with so many applicants, the government has rules and policies. The rules are supposed to be enforced without taking into account the applicant's race, religion, or gender. Applicants are selected according to their ability to adapt to Canadian life and to settle here successfully.

The government recognizes three classes of immigrants:

Family Class: Canadian citizens have the right to sponsor close relatives such as wives, husbands, fiancé(e)s, dependent sons or daughters, parents, grandparents, brothers, sisters, nephews, nieces, or grandchildren.

Immigration Classes

1992–1994

Classes of Immigrants	1992	1993	1994
Family (sponsored)	96 223	109 700	111 000
Refugees	36 608	24 800	28 300
Economic (independent)	87 946	111 300	110 700
Total	**220 770**	**245 800**	**250 000**

Source: Citizenship and Immigration Canada

1978–82

Hundreds of thousands of people flee from Vietnam, Laos, and Cambodia. Canada accepts more than 60 000 of the refugees.

1983

Unemployment in Canada keeps immigration rates low. Those who do arrive are usually relatives of people already living in Canada. They originate from almost every country in the world.

1992-93

Changes to immigration regulations are made, but the goal of Canada's program remains the same: to reunite families, protect refugees, and promote Canada's economic development.

1994

A new immigration policy is adopted. More emphasis is placed on the language, age, education, and work skills of immigrants rather than on reuniting families. Many more business people become immigrants.

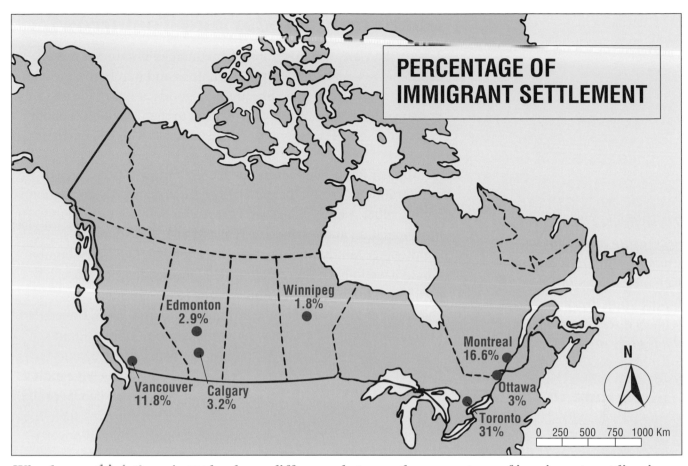

PERCENTAGE OF IMMIGRANT SETTLEMENT

Edmonton 2.9%

Winnipeg 1.8%

Vancouver 11.8%

Calgary 3.2%

Montreal 16.6%

Ottawa 3%

Toronto 31%

N

0 250 500 750 1000 Km

Why do you think there is such a large difference between the percentage of immigrants settling in eastern and western Canada?

Refugee: A person who has a well-founded fear of persecution for reasons of race, religion, political opinion, nationality, or membership in a social group.

Independent immigrants: This class includes assisted relatives, skilled workers, entrepreneurs, investors, and self-employed people.

Immediate family members and refugees receive the highest priority of all the applicants. There are three main reasons why Canada accepts immigrants:

Humanitarian: to fulfill international promises, to welcome desirable groups of people, and to unite families.

Economic: to build a prosperous country, to provide skilled people for the workforce, and to encourage economic development in all regions.

Social/Cultural: to encourage population growth and to build a strong, fair society.

At different times in the past, each of these reasons has been the most important one influencing immigration policy.

Immigrants to Canada tend to settle in three cities: Toronto, Montréal, and Vancouver. In Alberta, most newcomers settle in Edmonton or Calgary. Ontario attracts the largest number of immigrants. Even when they go to another province first, about eight percent eventually move to Ontario.

Making Choices

Decide why there have been dramatic changes in immigration from each of the source areas.

73

Immigration Today and Tomorrow

Today, the Canadian government encourages immigration for economic reasons. Immigrants create jobs and purchase Canadian goods and services. They also produce goods and provide services in many professions. Their contribution to the Canadian economy is considerable. They pay taxes that support the high Canadian standard of living.

Another important reason that the government encourages immigration is to help the population grow. Canada's population is getting older. Fewer babies are being born than are needed to keep the population at the same size. On average, Canadians have 1.2 children per family. In order to replace the parents, every family would have to have two children. This means that, for the population to grow, our birthrate needs to be more than two children per family. Since the birthrate is not that high, Canada's population would decrease without the addition of immigrants.

As the twenty-first century approaches, Canadians have built a country of which they can be proud. Canada is free of much of the violence, oppression, and poverty that plagues so many other countries. This is one important reason why so many people want to make Canada their home.

At the same time, Canada has several troubling problems, including racial tension in some areas. This tension, along with other barriers, prevents some people from participating fully in our society. In the following chapters, we will learn more about how we are developing new policies to promote harmony between communities.

These figures show the decreasing birth rate in Canada. Although Statistics Canada gathers this information every year, it takes a few years before the figures are published.

Birth Rate in Canada, 1921 – 1993

Year	Birth Rate Per 1 000 population
1921	29.3
1925	26.1
1930	23.9
1935	20.5
1940	21.6
1945	24.3
1950	27.1
1955	28.2
1960	26.8
1965	21.3
1970	17.5
1975	15.8
1980	15.5
1985	14.8
1990	15.2
1993	13.4

Source: Statistics Canada

Are business immigrants the best immigrants for Canada?

Business immigrants create jobs and are less likely to collect welfare or unemployment insurance than many other groups of Canadians.

Immigrants take jobs away from Canadians. They are willing to work for less pay.

Immigrants help build the workforce. They have many talents and skills that we need.

There is no evidence that immigrants are a drain on Canadian taxpayers. Business immigrants start businesses and create goods and services that we can sell.

During the latter half of the 1980s, twenty thousand business immigrants invested $3 billion and created 80 000 jobs in Canada.

Why should my country welcome immigrants when I can't find a job for myself?

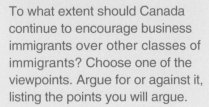

Making Choices ✔

To what extent should Canada continue to encourage business immigrants over other classes of immigrants? Choose one of the viewpoints. Argue for or against it, listing the points you will argue.

What Have We Learned

Immigration has played an important part in building Canada. Immigrants left their homes for a variety of reasons. Some came to Canada because life in their home country was unbearable due to poverty, war, or persecution. Others came because Canada was a land that held promise and hope for a better life. Government immigration policies have changed over the years. Today these government policies are guided by a desire to produce a strong Canadian economy.

Talk About

Discuss the many reasons immigrants came to Canada. What made certain immigrants more desirable than others in the eyes of the government? What impact do large numbers of immigrants have on people, facilities, and services?

Questions

1. Why is immigration important to Canada?
2. Why is immigration to Canada important to the immigrants?
3. How has Canada decided who will be welcomed as citizens?
4. Explain how immigration policy has changed over time.
5. How does Canada's birthrate affect Canada's immigration policies?

Activities

1. Create a timeline highlighting important events in Canada's immigration history.
2. Research a particular family or group that immigrated to Canada. List the reasons why they decided to come to Canada, and the reasons why Canada accepted them. Did your subjects assimilate to mainstream Canadian society, or did they remain segregated? Tell their story.
3. Design a concept cube. On each side of the cube, feature a particular group that came to Canada, and the contributions they made to Canadian culture.

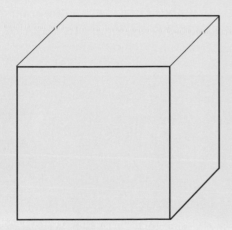

Skill Builders

1. Develop your graph-reading skills by using the declining birthrate chart on page 74 to answer the following questions:
   - In what year did Canada have the highest birthrate?
   - In what year was the birthrate the lowest?
   - Predict Canada's birthrate in the future.
   - What implications will your birthrate prediction have on immigration to Canada?
2. Prepare a skit featuring immigrant life in early Canada.
3. Develop your interviewing skills by interviewing a member of your family about your history. Extend the interview by doing some additional encyclopedia research to verify, or add to, the information you received.

Challenges

1. Defend a viewpoint from page 75 that differs from your own.
2. Describe what Canada might be like if the Europeans and other immigrants had not come to Canada.
3. Invent a fictional group of people who came to Canada. Describe their contributions.
4. Predict the future pattern of immigration to Canada. Draw a graph showing your predictions.

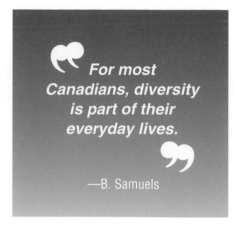

" For most Canadians, diversity is part of their everyday lives. "

—B. Samuels

5 Communities Today

anada is a country of many cultures, and all of these cultures play an important role in building the country. In earlier chapters, you read about Canada's "founding" communities, and you also read about immigrants who came from different countries to live here. In this chapter, you will study the impact that different cultural groups have on Canadian society.

Imagine a photograph so large that it includes every single Canadian citizen. Such a photograph would include people who are as different as the many countries from which they came. They would have their own ideas about education, business, health, and family, ideas as diverse as their backgrounds. All, however, are part of the Canadian community. They share more than the same location on the globe. They share a common desire to create the best way of life possible for themselves and their communities.

Our communities reflect the many cultural groups that now call Canada their home.

 Think About

Think about these facts when considering communities today:

- Eighty-two percent of Canadians live in neighbourhoods with people of different ethnic or racial backgrounds.
- Forty percent have family members with different ethnic or racial backgrounds.
- Sixty-four percent work with people from different ethnic or racial backgrounds.
- Seventy-three percent have friends they see regularly who have different ethnic or cultural backgrounds.

Although we are all part of Canadian society, each of us belongs to more than one community. A sports team, a club, a school, a religious group, a family— these are all communities to which we may belong.

Most people are involved in different types of communities at the same time. For example, you live on a street in a particular neighbourhood. That neighbourhood is part of a larger town or city, which is part of a province, which is part of Canada. Depending on the circumstances, you may identify yourself as belonging to one or more of these communities.

Each person contributes to a community in an individual way. In equal societies, all citizens enjoy the same chance to participate in community life. Our communities help us, teach us, guide us, and support us. In return, everyone has a responsibility to give something back to the community.

While all Canadians belong to Canadian society, each person belongs to other groups as well. Each Canadian participates in a number of different activities. These activities bring people with a variety of values, beliefs, and behaviours together in groups. Each group is a kind of community, sharing a common interest or bond. For example, you may belong to a club. The club may have rules of behaviour or a special dress code. You may also belong to a religious group in which certain beliefs and ways of behaving are expected. Each group to which you belong influences you in certain ways and contributes to making you the person you are.

A Boat Girl Grows Up

A Vietnamese Educates Coldwater

Decide whether the town of Coldwater, Ontario, helped Hang Truong become a part of its community, and whether her presence changed the town as well.

Even after ten years, Hang Truong has memories that make her wince. Among them is the recollection of one of the first mornings in her new home in Coldwater, a small Ontario town of 1 000 people not far from Orillia. The townspeople had given her a bicycle as a gesture of welcome. So Hang did what she would have done in her native Saigon. The result was not what she expected. "I think they were a little scandalized," she recalled with a shy smile. "I guess we were," agreed Jane Walker, a lifelong resident of Coldwater. "We just weren't accustomed to seeing a twenty-year-old girl riding around on a bicycle in her pyjamas." Hang was part of a wave of Southeast Asian "boat people" who found haven in Canada during the 1970s.

Hang, now married, is a mother and a budding entrepreneur. The town that opened its arms to her is no longer quite so surprised by her foreign habits and customs. Jane Walker belonged to a group of four Coldwater families that sponsored Hang and two of her young cousins. "It was very good for our little community here," she says. "It really broadened our horizons. In a place like this,

you know, contact with people of other races is not something that happens every day."

For Hang, it was a contact that might never have occurred at all if the Canadian government had not committed itself to a program to help the boat people in 1979. Like Hang, most of them were ethnic Chinese who fled from Vietnam after the war there ended in 1975. The program allowed four Coldwater families to form a sponsoring group, with the help of United Church minister Reverend John Allsop. They notified the government that they would help individuals with a low priority who might not otherwise have a chance of admission to Canada.

Hang was in that category. She was twenty years old, unmarried, had no relatives in Canada or knowledge of English or French, and was not particularly well-educated. In Vietnam, she had

The people of Coldwater supported Hang Truong and her family as they learned about Canadian life.

English language classes. In her class she met Du Truong, another refugee from Vietnam who arrived in Canada a week after she did. Two years later they were married.

The wedding was a major social event in Coldwater. For the ceremony, Hang wore a traditional Western white gown. After the ceremony, she changed into a traditional Chinese red silk dress.

Eventually the couple achieved modest prosperity. Hang continued to work, and her husband found a job at a Coldwater plant that manufactured plastic garbage bags. They took over the mortgage payments for the bungalow that their sponsors had bought, and soon owned it. They also had three children.

The children did not slow their pace. Five years after arriving in Canada, Hang and her family sold the Coldwater house and moved to Orillia where they now own a modest, but handsome home. Hang and Du are partners with Du's brother in a small block of furnished apartments. Hang and a Chinese girlfriend, an immigrant from Hong Kong, have plans to open a snack bar in Orillia. Says Hang: "We're calling it 'Genie.' It's magic, like the magic that brought me here."

Questions

1. Explain why Hang would consider it magic to come to Canada.
2. In what ways has Hang become like other Canadians? In what ways has she retained her own culture?
3. How did the people of Coldwater support Hang as a new immigrant?

helped her foster mother run a food stall in Saigon. What is more, she had two young cousins in her care—Ong Vi Truong, eight years old, and his brother Ming, fifteen. All three spent more than a year in a refugee camp in Malaysia.

It was while they were in Malaysia that fate intervened, in the form of the Coldwater sponsors. Besides agreeing to care for Hang and the boys for a year, the four Canadian families also pooled their money to make a downpayment on a bungalow. Others in town gave money to refurbish the house. "It was a real community effort," said Harold Wood, one of the four main sponsors.

Hang soon had two jobs—working ten hours a day at a florist shop, and extra hours at a local nursing home. At the same time, she was looking after the two boys, who were enrolled in Coldwater schools. Hang still found time to attend

Multicultural Communities

An ethnically- and culturally-diverse population offers many advantages to communities. Many immigrants bring a strong work ethic with them when they come to Canada, and they do not take their jobs for granted. Many also bring savings that they invest or use to start businesses of their own, thereby contributing to a healthy local economy.

One example of a Canadian city that has benefited from its ethnically-diverse population is Calgary, Alberta. People have lived in the Calgary area for at least 12 000 years. Archaeologists have found artifacts near the city dating back at least that far. Over the years, various Native groups lived in the area. The fur trade brought Europeans west to the Calgary region. American buffalo hunters and whisky traders built forts, one of which was located at the present site of Calgary. Settlement of the region brought the North-West Mounted Police to the area to keep the peace and stop the whisky trade. They built Fort Calgary in 1876. In 1883, the railway arrived, bringing people from all over the world to settle in the area of what is now Calgary.

Canada's future success will rely on a population that is well-educated and ethnically and culturally diverse.

Today about 800 000 people live in Calgary. About one fifth—approximately 160 000 people—were born in countries other than Canada. The ten most reported backgrounds of people in Calgary are: British, German, Ukrainian, Canadian, French, Chinese, Aboriginal, Dutch, Polish, and South Asian. So many of the new immigrants to Calgary are young adults that the city's average age is well below the national average. Much of Calgary's future success will depend on this young, well-educated, ethnically- and culturally-diverse population.

Communities Change

The great diversity in modern Canadian society is a sign of how communities change over time, and how people learn to adapt to change. Take, for example, Canada's Aboriginal Peoples. The arrival of European settlers changed their way of life forever. The newcomers tried to impose their own way of doing things on the Native Peoples, who suffered much hardship as a result. The Native Peoples accepted some of the new ways, but they refused to give up all of their own traditions, or to disappear as a separate people.

Today, Aboriginal communities are finding new strength in their traditional ways. Many desire to take more responsibility for their affairs, and to rely less on the government. They have called this process self-government, meaning that Aboriginal Peoples want more control of their own education, health, and legal systems. Aboriginal spokespeople such as Harold Cardinal, Elijah Harper, and Ovide Mercredi speak out for Aboriginal rights. Aboriginal communities are forging new relationships between themselves and the government.

During the past few years, Aboriginal Peoples have become more active in their desire for self-determination. Why do you think this has happened? What circumstances have changed?

In the past twenty years, Aboriginal Peoples have begun the process of creating their own laws, police forces, and education and justice systems. This is the foundation upon which self-government will be built. The federal government has already agreed with the idea of Aboriginal self-government. There still remains the challenge of working out what the idea means in detail. In part, it means the right to **self-determination**, which is the right to make their own choices about their future instead of having everything decided for them by government.

There are approximately 756 000 Canadians who are a member of one of Canada's Native Peoples, Inuit, or Métis, and their numbers are growing. It is expected that Saskatchewan's Aboriginal Peoples will double in number within the next twenty years, at which time they will make up fifteen percent of the provincial population. These people will continue to press their province and their country to help solve the problems that face their communities.

In 1975, the Indian Brotherhood of the Northwest Territories issued an important statement of rights called the Dene Declaration. The Indian Brotherhood represented the rights of both the Dene, who have treaty rights, and the Métis, who do not have treaty rights, although they are descendants of the Dene. Although the Indian Brotherhood no longer exists, both treaty and non-treaty Peoples are now represented by the Dene Nation.

Key Term

Self-determination is the right to make your own decisions about what is best for your community

The Dene Declaration: Statement of Rights

We the Dene of the N.W.T. insist on the right to be regarded by ourselves and the world as a nation.

Our struggle is for the recognition of the Dene Nation by the government and people of Canada and the peoples and governments of the world.

As once Europe was the exclusive homeland of the European peoples, Africa the exclusive homeland of the African peoples, the New World, North and South America, were the exclusive homeland of aboriginal peoples of the New World, the Amerindian and the Inuit.

Colonialism and imperialism is now dead or dying. Recent years have witnessed the birth of new nations or rebirth of old nations out of the ashes of colonialism.

As Europe is the place where you will find European countries with European governments for European peoples, now also you will find in Africa and Asia the existence of African and Asian countries with African and Asian governments for the African and Asian peoples.

The African and Asian peoples—the peoples of the Third World—have fought for and won the right to self-determination, the right to recognition as distinct peoples and the recognition of themselves as nations.

But in the New World, the Native Peoples have not fared so well. Even in countries in South America where the Native Peoples are the vast majority of the population, there is not one country which has an Amerindian government for Amerindian peoples.

Nowhere in the New World have the Native Peoples won the right to self-determination and the right to recognition by the world as a distinct people and as nations.

While the Native People of Canada are a minority in their homeland, the Native People of the N.W.T., the Dene and Inuit, are a majority of the population of the N.W.T.

The Dene find themselves as part of a country. That country is Canada. But the Government of Canada is not the government of the Dene. These governments were not the choice of the Dene, they were imposed on the Dene.

What we the Dene are struggling for is the recognition of the Dene Nation by the governments and peoples of the world.

And while there are realities we are forced to submit to, such as the existence of a country called Canada, we insist on the right to self-determination as a distinct people and the recognition of the Dene Nation.

We the Dene are part of the Fourth World. And as the peoples and nations of the world have come to recognize the existence and rights of those peoples who make up the Third World, the day must come and will come when the nations of the Fourth World will come to be recognized and respected. The challenge to the Dene and the world is to find the way for the recognition of the Dene Nation.

Our plea to the world is to help us in our struggle to find a place in the world community where we can exercise our right to self-determination as a distinct people and as a nation.

What we seek then is independence and self-determination within the country of Canada. This is what we mean when we call for a just land settlement for the Dene Nation.

Questions

1. What are the main points of the Dene Declaration?
2. According to the Declaration, what rights do the Dene people wish to obtain?

A New Community—A New Era

The struggle of the Aboriginal Peoples to take control of their own lives has come a long way in the past twenty years. One example of this is the creation of Nunavut, a new community created on May 26, 1993. On that day, Prime Minister Brian Mulroney went to the small village of Iqaluit on the shores of Frobisher Bay on Baffin Island, where he signed an agreement giving the Inuit People control of a territory larger than the three Maritime provinces combined.

By doing so, he set in motion the creation of Nunavut. When it is finally established, in 1999, Nunavut will join the Northwest Territories and the Yukon as Canada's third northern territory. At that time, Canada's map will change, something that has not happened since Newfoundland became a province in 1949.

In land area, Nunavut will be twice the size of British Columbia, although its population will be small.

Should the government negotiate land settlements with different Aboriginal groups? How will this affect the future of Canadian sovereignty?

The new territory of Nunavut will include many of Canada's Arctic islands. What are some potential problems facing this new territory?

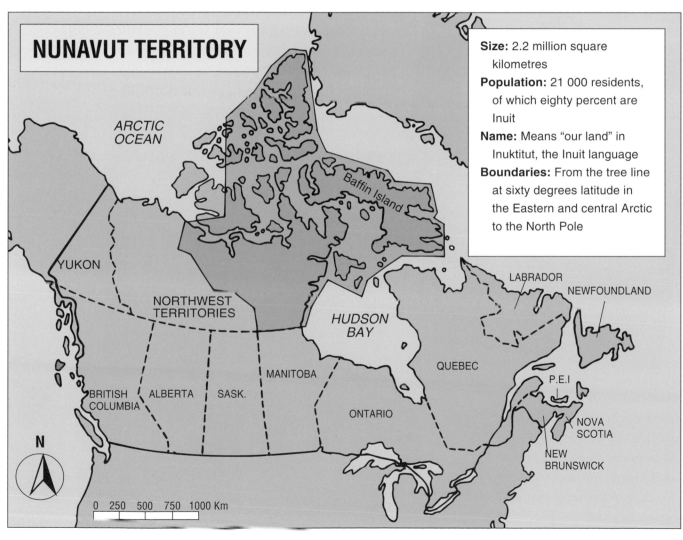

NUNAVUT TERRITORY

ARCTIC OCEAN

Baffin Island

YUKON

NORTHWEST TERRITORIES

HUDSON BAY

LABRADOR

NEWFOUNDLAND

BRITISH COLUMBIA

ALBERTA

SASK.

MANITOBA

QUEBEC

ONTARIO

P.E.I

NOVA SCOTIA

NEW BRUNSWICK

N

0 250 500 750 1000 Km

Size: 2.2 million square kilometres
Population: 21 000 residents, of which eighty percent are Inuit
Name: Means "our land" in Inuktitut, the Inuit language
Boundaries: From the tree line at sixty degrees latitude in the Eastern and central Arctic to the North Pole

Community Festivals

Like the Aboriginal Peoples, other groups within Canada try to keep their cultural traditions alive. For them, becoming Canadian does not mean that they have to give up all reminders of their heritage. Part of being Canadian is the ability to celebrate cultural diversity.

A community festival is one popular way to preserve cultural traditions. Many different groups across Canada put on festivals, which feature special foods and traditional clothing, dances, and songs. Even in today's busy world, communities take time to celebrate their heritage and cultural traditions.

In Alberta, people celebrate their Western heritage with events like the Calgary Stampede, Klondike Days in Edmonton, and the Buffalo Days Powwow and Tipi Village in Fort Macleod. The festival in Fort Macleod recalls the buffalo hunt in Aboriginal communities. A powwow commemorates the traditional site of the annual hunt, a high bluff over which the buffalo were stampeded to their death. Dance competitions, arts and crafts, and other activities celebrate the Aboriginal Peoples' traditional way of life.

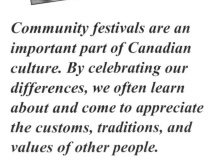

Community festivals are an important part of Canadian culture. By celebrating our differences, we often learn about and come to appreciate the customs, traditions, and values of other people.

In many cities across Canada, Chinese communities put on parades during their New Year's festivities in early February. Colourful dragons and ceremonial dances fill the streets. Many Chinese traditions are observed at this time. The banquet is a time for the whole family to get together to feast on a wide variety of special dishes. The variety of dishes at the banquet— be it ten or twenty— signifies completeness, an important theme in Chinese life. New Year's Cake is often served for dessert. It is round and made from a sweet, sticky rice. The shape of the cake symbolizes completeness, while the sweetness expresses the hope for a sweet new year. Fish is served because, to the Chinese, it means abundance or plenty. It is considered polite to serve the fish whole, with head and tail intact. By serving fish on New Year's Day, the family is expressing their hopes for food, money, health, and happiness in the year to come.

List some community festivals that occur in your area. Bring in pictures or items used in the celebrations. Describe what these festivals celebrate.

Christmas and Hanukkah are examples of community festivals that are based upon religious events. Decorating the Christmas tree with bright lights and giving gifts to friends and relatives are both examples of traditions that may have been in your family for years. During Hanukkah, a festival of lights, members of the Jewish community light candles in a "menorah," or candelabra, over a period of eight days. To celebrate Hanukkah, families exchange gifts and often donate money to charities.

Different festivals in Atlantic Canada recognize and celebrate the rich cultural heritage in that part of the country. The Annapolis Valley Apple Blossom Festival, for example, focusses on the agricultural heritage of Nova Scotia, while the Loyalist City Festival in Saint John, New Brunswick, acknowledges the Loyalist beginnings of that province. Perhaps the best-known Maritime festival is the Lucy Maud Montgomery Festival in Cavendish, Prince Edward Island. This is a festival of island life and culture that honours the works of island writer Lucy Maud Montgomery, author of the *Anne of Green Gables* stories.

Think About

Think about festivals celebrated by people in your community. What are some different kinds of celebration that you have participated in?

The Rankin Family

In the music industry, their kind of music is called "roots traditional." The Rankin Family's music is packed with Cape Breton culture— both the traditional and the modern. They are a living, breathing, singing, dancing example of what Cape Breton music is today.

All twelve Rankin children were born and raised on the west coast of Cape Breton Island, Nova Scotia, in a small town called Mabou, which is rich in Celtic culture. The family's Scottish and Irish ancestors came to Canada seven generations ago. The Rankins had their musicial beginnings as children, when all twelve performed for the locals. Over the years, various siblings have been involved in their performances, ending up with the current lineup of vocalists Raylene, Cookie, and Heather; singer, songwriter, and guitarist, Jimmy; and multi-instrumentalist, John Morris.

Much of the Rankins' appeal lies in their rich cultural heritage. Their success has come from playing the traditional music of their Scottish ancestors that has been blended with more modern influences. The group's first album, *The Rankin Family*, was released in 1989, and has since gone platinum. All of their recent albums have also been great successes. The Rankin Family is well-known for their popular live performances, and have played to sold-out concerts around the world. As part of their concert, they play fiddle tunes and sing ballads in the ancient Gaelic language of their ancestors.

In 1994, the Rankin Family won four Juno Awards for Group of the Year, the People's Choice Award for Canadian Entertainer of the Year, Single of the Year for "Fare Thee Well Love," and Country Group of the Year. The group has also won a dozen East Coast Music Awards, and has been nominated for many other awards. They have become extremely popular in Canada, and have increasingly attracted the attention of people internationally. By uniting the music of their cultural heritage with more contemporary music, they have introduced the Celtic sound to people around the world, and are well on their way to highly successful careers.

Making Choices

Do you believe that this type of Canadian culture will be accepted by other countries? Why or why not?

The Canadian Workplace Today

Cultural change can be a difficult process. Sometimes change occurs because people demand it. At other times, a new law is required to enforce change. In some cases, the government may insist on change by pressuring people and institutions to accept it. It is in this way that the government has the power to make positive changes in terms of human rights.

One way the government can enforce change is to hold back money from groups that do not follow government policies. This is the way the federal government began its **employment equity** program. Employment equity is designed to help specific groups of people get jobs. These groups are considered to be at a disadvantage in the competition for jobs, and employment equity is intended to help them compete equally with other, more privileged, groups.

Key Term

Employment Equity is a government program that attempts to make sure that jobs are open to all qualified people, regardless of their gender, skin colour, physical disability, racial background, or religious beliefs.

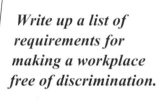

Write up a list of requirements for making a workplace free of discrimination.

It removes barriers so that more women, Aboriginal People, people with disabilities, and visible minorities can enter the workforce or can get promotions in their jobs.

When employment equity programs began, many organizations introduced them just so that they would not lose their government money. Employment equity programs are still very controversial. Some people claim that they are a form of "reverse discrimination." By this they mean that, instead of making everyone equal, employment equity makes it more difficult for people not included in the special groups to find jobs. They worry that employers who are encouraged to hire more women, more people from Aboriginal groups, more people with disabilities, and more visible minorities, will overlook other qualified people who do not fit into any of these categories.

Others argue that employment equity is equal treatment, not preferred treatment. By removing the barriers that some people face, they say, all qualified people have an equal opportunity to find work.

Today, partly because of the awareness of other cultures that multiculturalism encourages, employment equity is widely accepted in Canada.

What changes do you think are necessary in the workplace to allow all people to have equal opportunities?

Should governments regulate who gets a job?

We don't need the government telling us who to hire in our workplace. We have the right and the ability to choose the best person for the job.

I want to be judged on my abilities and my suitability for a job, not on my gender or my cultural background.

Whose role is it to judge whether a person should get a job, the government or the employer? Who knows best?

Employment equity has lessened my chance of getting a job because I am not a member of the target groups. I believe that is unfair.

Some people would not have jobs if the government did not have programs like employment equity. This program removes barriers.

Making Choices ✔

With which viewpoints do you agree? Debate the viewpoint question.

Chapter Review

5

What Have We Learned

Diversity is part of everyday life. Many of us live in communities with people of different cultural backgrounds. One way that we celebrate diversity is through community festivals where we find out about others, and learn to appreciate their values and traditional customs. Communities change over time as they adapt to changing circumstances. Sometimes changes happen on their own, and sometimes they are helped along by new laws and regulations.

 **Talk About**

The federal government is considering granting self-government to all Aboriginal Peoples. It is also closing many parts of the federal department of Indian Affairs. In small groups, discuss what these changes might mean for Aboriginal Peoples in the future.

?? Questions

1. How has Canada's immigration history and policies influenced communities in Canada today?
2. What is the major difference between self-government and self-determination?
3. Would you describe your community as culturally diverse? Explain, using examples.

Activities

1. As a class, write to the Chamber of Commerce in cities and towns across Canada to find out about interesting festivals in their communities. Create a wall calendar of community events and festivals. What do these festivals indicate about Canada's cultural heritage and diversity?

2. Create a description for a job of your choice. Role-play an interview with someone applying for the job. Be sure to ask fair questions that are sensitive to a person's cultural background. At the same time, the interview should be useful in finding out whether or not the applicant has the proper skills to do the job.

3. Brainstorm a list of all the people you know. Make the list as long as you can. After you have completed the list, begin to group the names into common categories: relatives, classmates, team members, people you see on the weekend, the friends you skateboard with, and so on. Place these groups of names into circles. Each circle represents a different community of people. How many communities do you belong to?

Skill Builders

1. Transfer the information from this graph onto a map of Canada. Make a colour-coded key showing the percentage of people living in racially/culturally diverse neighbourhoods in each province.

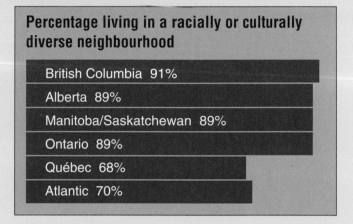

Percentage living in a racially or culturally diverse neighbourhood

British Columbia	91%
Alberta	89%
Manitoba/Saskatchewan	89%
Ontario	89%
Québec	68%
Atlantic	70%

a. Why do you think British Columbia has the most people living in racially or culturally diverse neighbourhoods?

b. Why do you think Québec and the Atlantic provinces have smaller percentages of people living in racially or culturally diverse neighbourhoods?

Challenges

1. Suppose Aboriginal Peoples win their right to self-government. Write about what difference it would make to their lives, and to Canada.

2. Compare the Dene Declaration on page 84 with the Métis List of Rights on page 59. How are the two similar? How do they differ?

Unit Three

Multiculturalism and Canadian Policies

6 Paving the Way

Canada has been a multicultural country since its beginnings—long before multiculturalism became a common word.

—B. Samuels

When European explorers and colonists arrived in North America, they found many different groups of Native Peoples living here. Each group had its own culture and spoke its own language. These original inhabitants, plus the colonists and the many immigrants who came later from all parts of the world, built a distinctive country called Canada.

Nation-building is a difficult task. Over the years, Canada has survived external threats and internal divisions. Every group in society did not always have the same rights. At certain times, some groups have dominated the others. For example, until 1960, Native Peoples were not allowed to vote in federal elections, a right most Canadians take for granted. Similarly, women could not vote in provincial elections in Québec until 1940, and Japanese Canadians could not vote federally until 1948. Over the years, all Canadians gradually received the same rights and responsibilities, but the process has been long and difficult.

Not until 1947 were citizens of Canada officially known as Canadians. Before that time, they were British subjects. The **Canadian Citizenship Act** brought about this change, and also raised the idea that immigrants and native-born Canadians should have the same rights.

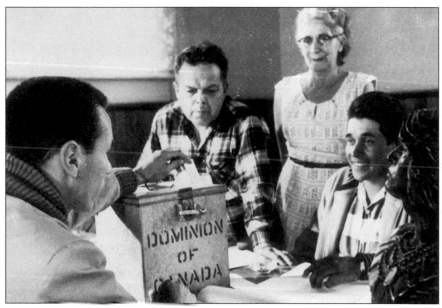

In the past, not all Canadian citizens have been treated equally or fairly when it came to voting rights. This photo shows members of the Rice Lake Band, in Ontario, some of the first Native Peoples allowed to vote, in 1960.

Key Term

The **Canadian Citizenship Act** describes who may become a citizen of Canada.

95

During the 1960s, three major trends helped to change the way Canadians thought about their society. These trends were:

1. Aboriginal Peoples began to demand a more active role in Canadian society.
2. People in Québec grew dissatisfied with their role in the Canadian federation.
3. Minority ethnic groups wanted a greater role in Canadian society.

These demands from three different groups posed difficult challenges to Canadian unity and identity. In 1963, Prime Minister Lester Pearson's government set up a Royal Commission on Bilingualism and Biculturalism to study the situation. The "B and B" Commission was asked to find ways of developing an equal partnership between French- and English-speaking Canadians. The Commission also considered the contributions of other cultural groups.

As a result of the Commission's work, the government passed the *Official Languages Act* in 1969, giving French and English equal status as the official languages of Canada. The act required the federal government to make its services available in both languages. This is what is meant when Canada is referred to as an officially bilingual country.

When newcomers arrive in Canada, they are expected to adopt one or both of the two official languages. To obtain Canadian **citizenship**, they must be able to speak one of these two languages. It is difficult for them to take part in Canadian society without some knowledge of French or English. Immigrants who are not able to speak one or the other of the official languages cannot find work easily, and cannot usually make as much money at their jobs. At the same time, of course, many immigrants also keep their original language, speaking it in the home and teaching it to their children.

By the 1980s, more than half the immigrants arriving in Canada were already able to speak at least one official language. For those who do not, language training is available, although it is not always easy for newcomers to learn a new language, especially if they are elderly or poorly-educated.

Of those immigrants who learn a new language, most outside Québec choose to learn English. They see English as the better language for getting a job and becoming a part of the larger North American community. Immigrants who settle in Québec must learn French because French is the common language in that province, but many learn English in addition.

Citizenship means belonging to and participating in your society, your country, your province and your community.

96

Announcing a New Policy—1971

A turning point in Canadian history occurred in 1971 when Prime Minister Pierre Elliott Trudeau made **multiculturalism** an official government policy. This marked the beginning of official multiculturalism, an important part of Canadian society today.

Prior to the new policy, Canada was considered a bicultural country in which British and French traditions formed the basis of society. Multiculturalism was a different way of looking at Canadian society. It recognized that there were many more groups than just the British and the French, and that these groups made valuable contributions to the country.

PROFILE

Pierre Elliot Trudeau

Although Pierre Elliot Trudeau had little experience in government before he became prime minister, his intelligence, charisma, and background in law and teaching helped him to succeed. In all, he was prime minister for almost fifteen-and-a-half years.

Trudeau is remembered for many achievements, especially in the areas of foreign policy and social reforms. Although he was from Québec himself, he had many fierce debates with Quebeckers about their status in Canada. He opposed the idea of a separate, independent Québec. Instead, he promised a "Just Society," meaning a society in which everyone has equal rights and equal opportunities. He wished to recognize the importance of all ethnic groups to Canadian life. In 1971, Trudeau and his government announced a new policy of multiculturalism.

In the House of Commons, Trudeau said that "such a policy would help to break down discriminatory attitudes and cultural jealousies. ...[A policy of multiculturalism] can form the base of a society which is based on fair play for all."

Multiculturalism gave official recognition to the diverse cultural groups that make up Canadian society. Trudeau encouraged immigrants to hold on to their native languages and customs. He felt that this would help all Canadians to become more aware of their country's rich cultural traditions.

Questions

1. Prime Minister Trudeau had to overcome opposition to his policy of multiculturalism. Do some research to find out the arguments of those who opposed the policy.
2. What were some of Prime Minister Trudeau's other accomplishments?

97

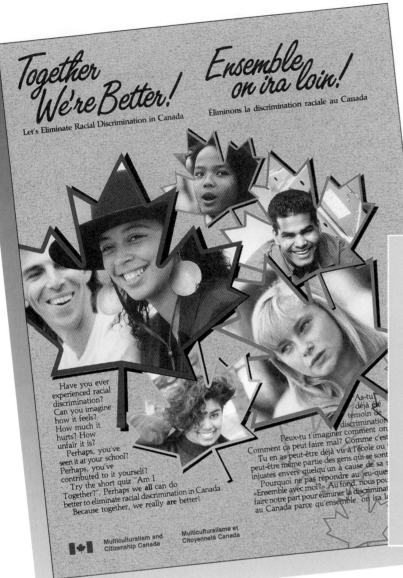

Of course, Canada did not suddenly become multicultural in 1971. Canadian society had been a mix of people with diverse backgrounds and traditions for a long time. In 1971, however, the government decided to make it official policy to promote and celebrate this diversity.

Prime Minister Trudeau's 1971 speech presented several main ideas. The most significant were:

- Canada has two official languages, French and English, but no official culture.
- No cultural group has special status over another.
- The government helps everyone to enjoy full participation in Canadian life.
- Diversity is encouraged within a framework of two official languages and a set of Canadian values shared by everyone.
- Multiculturalism upholds freedom of choice, the freedom to be different.

Why are we "better together," as the poster claims?

Trudeau stated that the government would support multiculturalism in four ways:

1. As long as resources allow it, the government will assist cultural groups to carry on their activities.

2. The government will assist members of all cultural groups in overcoming any barriers to full participation in Canadian society.

3. The government will promote contact between all cultural groups to encourage national unity.

4. The government will help immigrants to learn at least one of the official languages in order to become full participants in Canadian society.

Charter of Rights and Freedoms—1982

Other events during the next few years strengthened the role of multiculturalism in Canadian society. In 1982, the new Canadian constitution set out the Charter of Rights and Freedoms. The Charter guarantees equal rights to all Canadians, regardless of their cultural background. Placing these rights in the Charter made them easier to protect because they were supported by law rather than by tradition or popular opinion.

The Charter of Rights and Freedoms guarantees many **rights** to all Canadians, including:

- the right to vote
- the right to run for political office
- the right to enter and leave Canada at will
- the right to live and work anywhere in Canada
- the right for students to be educated in either official language, even if that language is not the language of the majority in the province
- the right to carry a Canadian passport
- the right to be considered first for some jobs

Along with rights come **responsibilities**. Responsibilities are what we owe the community in return for the privilege of living here. For example, Canadians have the responsibility to:

- take part in the political process by voting or running for office
- obey Canadian laws
- keep informed about public issues
- eliminate discrimination and injustice
- respect the rights of others
- respect private and public property
- preserve Canada's heritage
- support Canadian values
- strengthen communities

Key Term

Rights are things to which people are entitled. Many rights are protected by law.
Responsibilities are obligations that we owe to other people and to our community.

Official Multiculturalism—1988

In 1988, Parliament **unanimously** adopted the *Multiculturalism Act*, making Canada the first country in the world to have an official policy of multiculturalism. Addressed to all Canadians, the new policy was based on the idea that everyone is responsible for changes in society. This responsibility includes the elimination of racism and discrimination.

The main principles of the *Multiculturalism Act* are:

- Multiculturalism is a basic fact of Canadian society.
- Diverse cultures and languages should be preserved, strengthened, and integrated into Canadian society.
- All Canadians should work to eliminate discrimination and increase understanding of different cultures.

The government declared that its policies would promote the full and equal participation of all citizens in Canadian society. The government also said it would make sure that everyone received equal treatment and protection under the law.

Unanimously means that everyone is in complete agreement.

As this pie chart shows, Canadians generally support the policy of multiculturalism. Take a poll to find out how your classmates feel about it. Use the results to make a pie chart like this one.

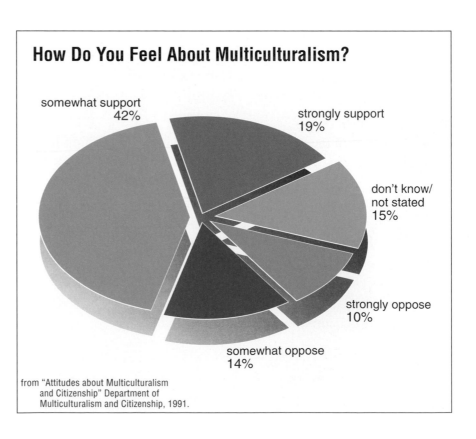

How Do You Feel About Multiculturalism?

somewhat support
42%

strongly support
19%

don't know/
not stated
15%

strongly oppose
10%

somewhat oppose
14%

from "Attitudes about Multiculturalism and Citizenship" Department of Multiculturalism and Citizenship, 1991.

What is Citizenship?

Anyone born in Canada is automatically a Canadian citizen. New immigrants to Canada must apply to become citizens. Citizenship gives Canadians the right to participate in and contribute to Canadian life. Being a Canadian citizen means having the freedom to choose how to participate in Canadian culture.

Citizenship does not give special privileges to only a few people, but gives equal rights to any person who qualifies to be a Canadian citizen. All Canadian citizens have the same rights, such as the right to vote, and the right to run as candidates in elections. Citizenship gives Canadians the right to travel abroad, and to return to Canada. Some jobs, especially government positions, and some scholarships and funding for students or businesspeople are only available to Canadian citizens.

Citizenship means being loyal to Canada, and being committed to certain values that Canadian citizenship supports. It also means having certain responsibilities to the country and to your community.

Think About

Why do you feel at home in your own country?

Canadian citizenship is a right, but it is also a set of responsibilities. What responsibilities might these new Canadian citizens undertake?

How We Think About Ourselves

The beginning of the Canadian Constitution states the goal of "Peace, Order and Good Government," a phrase first used in 1867 by the Fathers of Confederation. In a very general way, these words sum up the aims of the Canadian government. They also create images of what it means to be a Canadian citizen. In contrast, the American constitution states the national goal of "Life, Liberty, and the Pursuit of Happiness." These words bring to mind quite different images.

People born in Canada are automatically Canadian citizens. Immigrants to the country must go through a process of becoming a Canadian citizen. This is called naturalization. Find out how a newcomer goes about becoming a Canadian citizen. What happens at a citizenship ceremony?

When newcomers become citizens, they become part of Canadian culture. They are expected to accept Canadian laws and to promote the values and beliefs held by most Canadians. Both native-born and naturalized Canadians enjoy the same rights and have the same obligations of citizenship.

Every year, during National Citizenship Week, special ceremonies and events remind Canadians of their rights and duties as citizens.

Citizen Participation

Allcitizens are expected to participate in Canadian life by fulfilling the responsibilities of citizenship.

It is common for societies to celebrate their heroes. Role models set examples for other Canadians, and help to pass on cultural values from one generation to the next. Religious leaders, sports champions, politicians, war heroes, and individuals who have performed courageous deeds are all honoured for doing something extraordinary.

Canadians are sometimes accused of being too modest, and of not recognizing individual achievement. Canadian heroes are often better known outside of Canada. Some people believe that this reluctance to recognize our heroes and to celebrate their efforts discourages attempts to build a strong Canadian culture. Do you agree?

There are many people in our communities who are not necessarily famous, but who do things that are above and beyond what is expected of them. Even though they may not receive a medal or an award, they are heroes nonetheless. Here are stories about three special Canadians who have made a difference.

David See-Chai Lam

David See-Chai Lam, British Columbia's former lieutenant-governor, is one of Canada's most successful immigrants. He, his wife Dorothy, and their three daughters left Hong Kong for Vancouver in 1967. Since then he has made a great deal of money in real estate, much of which he has given away to worthy causes. In 1988, he

was named British Columbia's lieutenant-governor, the Queen's representative in that province. During his years in office, he tried to increase understanding between established Canadians and new arrivals. "It's quite natural for people to feel uncomfortable with people who are different from themselves," he says.

Lam tells Canadians that they should not be quite so proud of their reputation for tolerance. "Tolerance is a slightly negative word," he says. "It's like saying, 'You smell, but I can hold my breath.'" He would like Canada to celebrate its immigrants, not just put up with them.

Lam is tougher on the newcomers, however. He has little patience for complaints about minor incidents of discrimination. "Don't talk to me about discrimination," he says bluntly. "The Chinese race is one of the most discriminatory in the world. I say to them, 'Do you think you will live to see the day when in one of the provinces in China, or in any of the countries in Asia, there will be a blond, blue-eyed governor?'" He also speaks against the common practice among elderly Chinese Canadians of having their bodies sent back to China for burial. "I tell them to go out and buy a burial plot in Vancouver," he says. "That's when they'll really be committed to Canada."

In his attempts to end cultural misunderstanding, Lam tries to explain the customs of one group to the other. Simple misunderstandings sometimes create antagonism. For example, he points out that the Canadian custom of going door-to-door selling things like Girl Guide cookies or collecting donations for school projects is misunderstood by the Chinese. "Chinese people think that if someone comes to the door and asks for money, they are a beggar, and they send them away." He explains the custom to new arrivals so they will not offend the youngsters—and their parents. Lam thinks that his greatest contribution has been his becoming lieutenant-governor. "British Columbia has a long, long history of discrimination," he says. "To have someone of the Chinese race now occupying its most important residence, that says a lot." To both sides.

Lennett Anderson

In October 1992, Lennett Anderson, a Grade 11 student in Nova Scotia, was stunned to see leaflets headlined "KKK White Power Lives!" circulating around his school. KKK refers to the Ku Klux Klan, a White supremacist group. One of about thirty Blacks among nearly 1 200 students, Lennett noticed that the leaflets were creating a lot of tension at the school. As president of the Cultural Awareness Youth Group, an organization that meets weekly to discuss racial issues and promote harmony, he invited students to an assembly where they expressed their feelings and agreed that "we need to get along." Lennett also pushed the school to make changes to its curriculum, such as including a course in Black Literature.

His teachers say that Lennett is a "positive role model—a good student and very helpful in promoting harmony." He is also an active church member, a sea cadet, and was a member of the Nova Scotia Board of the Children's Wish Foundation. "We are all equal," he says, "and should treat each other accordingly."

Gordon Mayer

Gordon Mayer knows firsthand the stings of racial discrimination. "Acceptance by others is a problem facing Aboriginal youth," says the nineteen-year-old Swampy Cree, who lives in Manitoba. When he saw the problems youngsters from his area were getting into, he wondered whether he would go the same way. Instead he decided to "get involved." He became a youth delegate on the board of directors of The Pas Friendship Centre, where he spends much of his spare time helping others. He also volunteers as a piano and vocal teacher, and is the only teenage member of the community's justice committee, which helps young offenders.

Besides his studies and volunteer work, Gordon has two part-time jobs—one in a clothing store, and the other with Native Child and Family Services. Gordon is a peer counsellor, helping young people cope with their problems. He discusses things such as self-esteem and motivation, believing that young people feel more comfortable talking to someone their own age. "I take kids out for a good time to talk to them and keep them out of trouble. I show them they are welcome by somebody. Some kids can't handle facing prejudice—they get mad. I think people should talk more about prejudice instead of just standing there doing nothing and being part of the problem rather than the solution."

Questions

1. On a map of Canada, locate where these three special Canadians live.
2. What qualities do they have in common?
3. Think up a inspirational title for each story.
4. What are three wise comments mentioned in the stories?

What does multiculturalism mean to you?

Multiculturalism enriches Canada's culture. I highly support it.

Multiculturalism destroys the fabric of Canadian society. It creates problems rather than solving them. It forces Canada to change too quickly.

Multiculturalism helps unite Canada as a country. It's a strong force that brings us together.

Multiculturalism enflames discrimination against non-whites. It creates conflict between groups.

Multiculturalism promotes foreign trade with other countries. We should keep an official multiculturalism policy. It's good for the economy.

Making Choices ✓

What is your attitude toward multiculturalism? What or who has influenced the way you feel about multiculturalism?

What We Have Learned

Canada was the first country in the world with an official multiculturalism policy. There were a number of steps to create this policy. First, the *Canadian Citizenship Act* (1947) led people to think about immigrants and native-born Canadians as having the same rights. Then the *Official Languages Act* (1969) gave French and English equal status as official languages. In 1971, Prime Minister Pierre Trudeau declared the value of a multicultural society. Ten years later, the Charter of Rights and Freedoms strengthened the place of multiculturalism in Canada. Finally, the *Canadian Multiculturalism Act* was adopted in 1988.

Talk About

What are some of Canada's ideals? Discuss the difference between a right and a responsibility.

Questions

1. What events in Canadian history have paved the way for the *Multiculturalism Act*?
2. Name the prime minister who made multiculturalism a national policy. Outline the intent of the policy.
3. What did the Canadian Charter of Rights and Freedoms do for Canadians?
4. Summarize different Canadian attitudes towards multiculturalism.

Activities

1. Select an issue concerning Canada's multiculturalism policy. Find newspaper articles that present contrasting views on the issue. Write an editorial expressing your own point of view.
2. Look for newspaper or magazine articles that discuss the rights and responsibilities of Canadians. Begin a class scrapbook or make a class display.
3. Work with your classmates to develop a list of the rights and responsibilities of members of your class.
4. Draw a picture or make a poster illustrating your understanding of the policy of multiculturalism. At the bottom of your picture, write the phrase from the policy that best describes the picture.

Skill Builder

1. Use your drawing skills to create a poster. Divide the poster into two parts. Write the words "Peace, Order, and Good Government" in the top half, and in the bottom half write "Life, Liberty, and the Pursuit of Happiness." Draw some of the images that these phrases bring to mind.
2. Use an atlas of Canada to find the distribution of French and English languages in each region of the country. Draw a map showing this distribution.
3. Break into groups and have each group choose an individual from your school or community who is a special citizen. Explain why they deserve special recognition. Design certificates of thanks and arrange a special ceremony to present the certificates to them during National Citizenship Week, held in February each year.

Challenges

1. Break into groups and discuss the strengths of Canada's multiculturalism policy.
2. If you were going to write a new *Citizenship Act* for Canada, what might it say?
3. Predict the future of multiculturalism in Canada. Prepare a list of questions Canadians need to address in order to ensure the survival of multiculturalism.

7 The Symbols of Canada

Multiculturalism is a policy that welcomes, even celebrates, cultural diversity. "It is a question of personal freedom," said Prime Minister Trudeau when he introduced the policy. Multiculturalism leaves us "free to be ourselves," he said, free to be different.

Many people still object to this way of describing Canada. They believe that a strong country needs a single, uniform culture. They argue that it is difficult to build a nation when there are so many different ideas about how the nation should develop. For instance, some Canadians continue to believe that Canada is fundamentally a partnership between the French and the English, while others prefer to think of Canada as a mosaic of many cultures.

A nation consists of a group of people who share similar ideas about themselves and their community. Often these ideas, or values, are expressed in symbols. These symbols are important expressions of the nation's identity. As a country changes over the years, so does its identity; and as the country's identity changes, so do its symbols.

The repatriation of our constitution was an important event in Canadian history. Find out what repatriation means. Why was Queen Elizabeth II involved? What changes did this event bring?

Changing Symbols

Throughout its history, Canada has adopted symbols to represent itself as a nation. National symbols are recognized at home and around the world. These symbols embody the things we value about our country. Because they represent something so important to us, changes to our symbols often result in debate and disagreement.

The flag is an example of a symbol that sparked great debate. Since Confederation, Canada did not have a flag of its own. Instead its flag was the British flag, the Union Jack. Attempts were made to change the flag, but each attempt failed. Many Canadians felt that having a unique flag meant breaking an important tie with Britain. In 1963, Prime Minister Lester Pearson raised the idea again. Controversy raged over what the new flag should look like. Finally Parliament approved the now-familiar red maple leaf design. The new flag was officially adopted on February 15, 1965. Today it is one of Canada's most popular and recognized symbols.

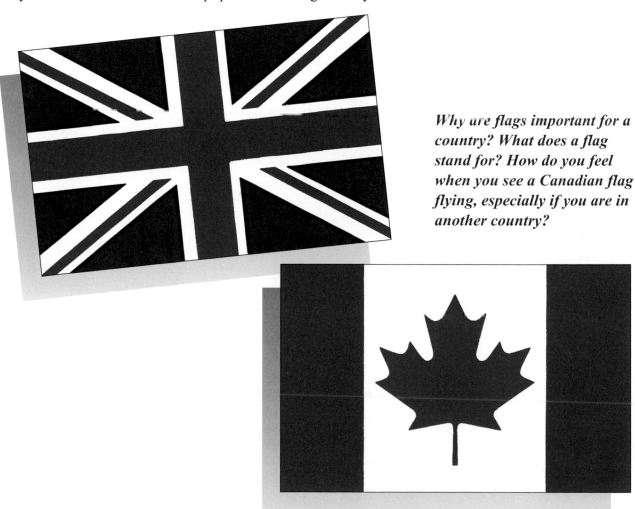

Why are flags important for a country? What does a flag stand for? How do you feel when you see a Canadian flag flying, especially if you are in another country?

Should Canada break ties with the British monarchy?

Canada has strong ties to Britain. To sever these ties would be like breaking up a family. I do not support Canada turning her back on Britain.

I respect the British monarchy, but I also recognize that Canada has grown and developed since her ties with Britain were established. Canada needs to break away to become a mature nation.

The British monarchy has only a ceremonial presence in Canada. I don't think it matters one way or the other if they are or are not a part of the Canadian scene.

Canada has had many opportunities to break away from Britain. For example, when the Americans revolted, we had the same opportunity, but we did not do it. At every opportunity, Canadians have affirmed their loyalty to the British Crown. If given the choice, I believe Canadians would again support their British connections.

As a Canadian without British roots, the monarchy means nothing to me. Canada needs to let go of these ties and cultivate an image more representative of its people.

Making Choices ✔

Come to a personal decision on whether Canada should break ties with the British monarchy.

Symbols and Meanings

Every culture has important symbols that give meaning to its customs and traditions. Some symbols are widely recognized. Examples include the cross as a symbol of Christianity, the Star of David for Judaism, and the Crescent for the Muslim religion. Country flags are another symbol that are widely recognized around the world.

Even things like colours or animals can sometimes be symbolic. For the Chinese, red symbolizes joy, festivity, and good luck. For some people, a black cat or raven symbolizes bad luck. An owl is considered a symbol of wisdom for Western cultures, but means foolishness in India.

Each object, colour, or event that is recognized by a group of people as symbolic of themselves has great meaning for them. It represents things in which they strongly believe. This is why immigrants to Canada often retain the traditional symbols of their homeland. As time passes and they become more at home in Canada, they usually adopt Canadian symbols as well.

Symbols Chart

Eye		The eye is all-seeing; it gives protection against evil	Egyptian Middle Eastern
Bee		Life-giving	Slavic Roman
Dragon		Life-giving	Chinese
Snarling Jaguar		Supernatural power	Olmec Peru
Fish		Rebirth	Slavic Indo-European
Cherry Tree		Rebirth	Chinese Japanese
Lotus		Perfection	South East Asian Indian Bangladeshi
Peacock		Eternity	Middle Eastern South East Asian
Snake		Regeneration	Ancient India
Circle		Universe	Slavic Ukrainian

Canadian Symbols

Let us take a closer look at some Canadian symbols. They help us represent ourselves to the rest of the world, and provide a common cultural reference for one another. What do our symbols say to others about us as Canadians? What makes Canadians different from similar people, such as our American neighbours?

Canadian symbols that come quickly to mind are the flag and the national anthem, "O Canada." Flags identify countries and serve as an image of what that country represents. Many Canadians who travel abroad display the red maple leaf on their luggage because they know Canada has a good reputation in the world. People are very proud of their flags. Since the flag symbolizes a country, destroying or damaging a flag is considered a very serious crime as it symbolizes the destruction of the country.

"O Canada" is another symbol of Canada. It was first performed in June 1880. Calixa Lavallée, a Québec musician, wrote the music, and the first words were written in French by Adolphe-Basile Routhier. In 1908, Robert Stanley Weir created English words for the music. "God Save the Queen" remained the official anthem, but Canadians sang "O Canada" on many occasions anyway. In 1980, one hundred years after it was written, Parliament declared "O Canada" to be the new official anthem of Canada.

♫ O Canada

O Canada! Our home and native land!
True patriot love in all thy sons command.
With glowing hearts we see thee rise,
The True North strong and free!
From far and wide, O Canada,
We stand on guard for thee.
God keep our land glorious and free!
O Canada, we stand on guard for thee.
O Canada, we stand on guard for thee.

Ô Canada! Terre de nos aïeux,
Ton front est ceint de fleurons glorieux!
Car ton bras sait porter l'épée,
Il sait porter la croix!
Ton histoire est un épopée
Des plus brilliants exploits,
Et ta valeur, de foi trempée,
Protégera nos foyers est nos droits,
Protégera nos foyers est nos droits.

Canadian symbols come from many places. Some originate from our unique history. The beaver, for example, became a symbol of Canada because the fur trade was important for so many years. The land is another source of symbols. Few countries have the grandeur, variety, and beauty of the Canadian landscape. The maple leaf itself is a symbol that originated in the landscape. Another source of symbols were the Aboriginal Peoples. The totem pole and the canoe, two important elements of Aboriginal culture, have become symbolic of Canada to many people.

The Canadian form of government is also unique. It is a democratic parliamentary system that combines elements of both the British and American systems. Our Parliament is a symbol of Canada's heritage and uniqueness.

Canada has an image as a nation devoted to world peace. Canadian soldiers have often been called upon to help keep the peace in other countries torn by conflict. The peacekeeper has become an important Canadian symbol.

Do you cheer for Canadian teams when they compete at international events? How do you feel when they win?

Canadian laws provide another reflection of Canada. Laws embody what most Canadians believe is the right and proper thing to do. For example, Canadian gun laws are more restrictive than American laws. Many Canadians who support these gun laws believe they symbolize a more peaceful, law-abiding society.

Sports offer yet another source of symbols and pride. For example, Canadians are identified around the world with the game of hockey.

Obviously, there is no single image or symbol that means Canada to everyone. Canada's image includes all of these symbols, and more.

Symbols and Traditions

Symbols, and the traditions they embody, change over time. Holidays are one example. Canadians celebrate Victoria Day in May each year. This holiday honours Queen Victoria, but many people wonder why Canadians should continue to celebrate the birthday of a British queen. Sunday shopping is another example. At one time Canadians could not shop on Sunday. It was considered a holiday, and all stores were closed. In most places it was illegal for shopkeepers to open even if they wanted to. Traditions have changed, however, and in most parts of Canada today Sunday shopping is allowed.

The Royal Canadian Mounted Police is another changing symbol. The RCMP was created in 1873 and became a symbol of justice for many Canadians. When the force began hiring more women and members of visible minorities, changes to some long-held traditions had to be made. Sometimes the changes have been controversial. The issue of whether or not traditional Aboriginal braids, Sikh turbans, and women's skirts should be part of the RCMP uniform has been hotly debated.

Constable Debbie Flintoff of the North Vancouver RCMP is a Cree from the Saddle Lake Band in Alberta. As of September 1995, she had served with the RCMP for seventeen years. How has Constable Flintoff contributed to changing Canadian traditions?

Think About

Consider other Canadian symbols that have changed or may change in your lifetime.

The Sikh Turban

Canadian traditions and symbols sometimes change to accommodate different cultures.

Hats, caps and toques are all examples of headgear designed to be worn outdoors against the cold and rain. It is considered good manners to remove a hat, or at least to lift it slightly, when greeting someone. Normally a hat, like a coat, is removed upon going indoors before joining polite company.

What about crowns, mitres, mortarboards, and robes? Are they also supposed to be respectfully removed in the company of others? Not usually. They are different. They are regalia: royal, religious, or learned symbols with a function quite unrelated to the weather or to fashion.

During the past few years, there has been a dispute at certain Royal Canadian Legion branches over whether to allow people of the Sikh religion to keep their turbans on inside the Legion

halls. Some Legion members say that out of respect all headgear must be removed. Sikhs answer that their turbans are not hats, but religious symbols. The case presents an interesting cultural conflict that is hard to understand without some background on what the turban means to the Sikhs.

The Sikh religion was founded in northern India during the fifteenth century, a period of frequent warfare between invading Muslim Moghul people and the local Hindu kingdoms. The Sikhs formed a small religious community that struggled to hold its own for several centuries against oppression by foreign rulers. The tenth religious leader, or guru, of the Sikhs, Guru Gobind Singh, understood that the Sikhs needed a disciplined nationalist defence force of "saint soldiers" in order to survive. In 1699, he created the new Order of the Khalsa, or Sikh Brotherhood of the Pure, which helped the

A turban is a piece of cotton material roughly five to six metres long and more than a metre wide. It is loosely pleated at both ends before it is tied around the head.

Sikh community gain a strong and lasting presence in the Punjab region of India.

Members of the new order had to be baptised, much like confirmation in the Catholic Church. Members of the Khalsa take religious vows and adopt certain lifestyle rules. They are required to wear five objects that symbolize the main Sikh beliefs. These objects are called the Five Ks, because their names in Punjabi all start with K.

One of these symbols is that a person's hair should never be cut or shaved. This is called keshas. In India, long hair means moral and spiritual strength, and is associated with saintliness. The Sikhs' long hair must be neatly groomed and tied into a knot on the top of the head where it is covered by the turban. The turban is considered the religious crown of the Sikh. A baptised man is under a vow to cover his long hair and to wear a turban in public at all times. For someone to request its removal, or worse to knock it off, is to show serious disrespect. It is not as simple as asking someone to take off a hat; it is asking someone to break a religious vow.

It is important to remember that a turban and long hair always go together. A Sikh with short hair is under no obligation to wear a turban. The debate about the turban and the Legion only concerns orthodox Sikhs.

The turban is a traditional form of headwear for Sikhs. Research other kinds of headwear and explain their significance.

Making Choices

Decide whether you support the following argument. Over the years, the uniform of the RCMP has evolved. Fashion has had something to do with it, but so have people. When women became part of the force, for example, certain changes were made to the uniform. If the uniform changed for women, why should it not be changed for others?

Borrowing Traditions

Canadian culture is constantly evolving, borrowing, and adopting from other cultures. Useful elements of other cultures become part of the Canadian way of life. A good example of this process from Canada's early history is the many items of Aboriginal culture that became part of everyday life for European settlers. Ideas and customs were shared, exchanged, and eventually absorbed into the mainstream culture.

The subject of culture has fascinated **anthropologists** for a long time. While investigating cultures around the world, they have made some important discoveries that help us to understand how our own culture developed. No culture develops in isolation. Many everyday things that we take for granted as belonging exclusively to our way of life have been borrowed from other cultures.

Anthropologists are people who study other cultures.

Aboriginal Peoples have long used canoes as an efficient way to travel on rivers and lakes. Canoes are just one example of an idea or custom assimilated by fur traders and other early settlers to Canada.

The Origins of Canadian Culture

The distinguished American anthropologist Professor Ralph Linton wrote about culture some forty years ago in his book, *The Study of Man*. To make his point, he told a story of a young American's ignorance of the effect other cultures had on his daily life. Here is a similar story that gives an interesting perspective on the origins of Canadian culture.

Our solid Canadian citizen, whom we shall call Richard, wakes up in a bed built on a pattern that originated in the Near East, but was modified in northern Europe before it was transmitted to North America. He throws back covers made from cotton, domesticated in India, or linen, domesticated in the Near East, or from sheep's wool, also domesticated in the Near East.

He goes to the bathroom, whose fixtures are a mixture of European and American inventions—of recent date. Richard then takes off his pyjamas, a garment from India, and washes with soap invented by the ancient Gauls. He then shaves, a rite which seems to have been derived from either Sumer or ancient Egypt.

Returning to his bedroom, he proceeds to dress. He puts on garments whose form originally derived from the skin clothing of the nomads of the Asiatic steppes, puts on shoes made from skins tanned by a process invented in ancient Egypt and cut from a pattern derived from the classical civilizations of the Mediterranean, and ties around his neck a strip of brightly coloured cloth that recalls the shoulder shawls worn by seventeenth-century Croatians. Before going

out for breakfast, he glances through the window made of glass invented in Egypt, and if it is raining, he puts on overshoes made of rubber discovered by the Central American Indians, and takes an umbrella, invented in Southeastern Asia. Upon his head, he places a hat made of felt, a material invented on the Asiatic steppes.

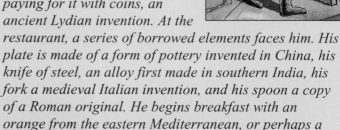

Richard walks down McGregor Street on his way to breakfast. He buys a paper, paying for it with coins, an ancient Lydian invention. At the restaurant, a series of borrowed elements faces him. His plate is made of a form of pottery invented in China, his knife of steel, an alloy first made in southern India, his fork a medieval Italian invention, and his spoon a copy of a Roman original. He begins breakfast with an orange from the eastern Mediterranean, or perhaps a cantaloupe from Persia, or maybe a piece of African watermelon. He has a cup of coffee, an Abyssinian plant, with cream and sugar. Both the domestication of cows and the idea of milking them began in the Near East, while sugar was first made in India. After this he goes on to waffles, cakes made by a Scandinavian technique, from wheat domesticated in Asia Minor. Over these he pours maple syrup, invented by the Native Peoples of the Eastern Woodlands. As a side dish, he may have an egg of a species of bird domesticated by Indo-China, or thin strips of the flesh of an animal domesticated in Eastern Asia, which have been salted and smoked by a process evolved in northern Europe.

Making Choices

What lesson did you learn from this story? Like Richard, do you use items that have come from other cultures? Select several items from your everyday life and research where they have come from.

Prayer in the House of Commons

Since 1877, Members of Parliament have recited a prayer at the start of their day in the House of Commons. In 1994, this tradition was challenged as not being in keeping with the multicultural nature of Canada. Here are four points of view expressed by MPs during the recent debate on the issue:

- The prayer is a Christian tradition, and Parliament should avoid creating an impression that any religion is the "official" Canadian religion.
- MPs should have more important things to do with their time than fuss about prayers when the country faces some huge problems.
- The prayer should be replaced by a minute of silence. That way everyone could pray in their own way, showing that Canada is a place of different races, cultures, and religions working together toward a common goal.
- Canada was founded as a Christian country, and the daily prayer is part of our history and traditions. We should not have to change what we are. Canadians going to live in other countries do not expect these countries to follow their traditions.

> Almighty God:
> We give thanks for the great blessings which have been bestowed on Canada and its citizens, including the gifts of freedom, opportunity and peace that we enjoy. We pray for our sovereign, Queen Elizabeth, and the Governor General. Guide us in our deliberations as Members of Parliament, and strengthen us in our awareness of our duties and responsibilities as Members. Grant us wisdom, knowledge, and understanding to preserve the blessings of this country for the benefit of all and to make good laws and wise decisions.
> Amen.

The prayer included such phrases as "O Lord our heavenly Father, high and mighty, King of kings, Lord of Lords," and "Most heartily we beseech thee with thy favour to behold our gracious sovereign lady, Queen Elizabeth; and so replenish her with the grace of thy holy spirit." There were also references to God and Jesus Christ.

MPs had different reasons for objecting to the prayer. Some Bloc Québécois MPs, who believe in an independent Québec, had difficulty accepting references to the British Queen. Other MPs who were not Christians felt that there might be a more appropriate prayer that would be more acceptable to all MPs. At the same time, there were MPs who did not want the prayer changed. They thought that it reminded Canadians of their origins as a Christian nation.

The debate was heated, and eventually a new prayer was adopted. The new version makes no reference to any one religion, and it is followed by a moment of silence. The changes were summed up by one Canadian: "The new prayer may not please everyone, but it does affirm the diversity of the Canadian people. National institutions have to reflect national realities."

MPs in the House of Commons now recite this prayer at the start of their day.

Think About

Reflect on the following:

- Thirteen percent of the population of Canada in 1994 was non-Christian.
- Between 1981 and 1991, the number of people in Canada practising non-Christian Eastern religions grew by 144 percent. Those religions include Hinduism, Buddhism, Sikhism, and Islam.

Bilingualism in Québec

As you have learned, Canada is officially a **bilingual** country. Of the ten provinces, Québec is the only one with a majority of French-speaking people. Over the past twenty years, French-speaking Quebeckers have grown concerned about protecting their rights as a minority in Canada, where most people speak English.

The Québec government was alarmed at the tendency of new immigrants to learn English instead of French. Wishing to preserve the French language and culture, in 1977 the Québec government passed a law known as Bill 101. This bill limits the use of any language other than French in Québec. It says that immigrants coming to Québec must send their children to French-language schools. If the immigrants remain in Québec to live, they must learn to speak French.

In 1988, the province passed another bill. Bill 178 banned the use of any language other than French on outdoor commercial signs. Many English-speaking Quebeckers felt that this law discriminated against them and their right to use their own language, which was after all an "official" language of Canada. Bill 178, the so-called "sign law," created controversy across Canada about the rights of the individual and the use of language.

The majority of people arriving in Québec each year to live do not speak French. People coming there who speak neither French nor English have been called **allophones**. *Allos* means "other" in Greek; an allophone speaks a language other than English or French.

Some new Canadians resist learning the French language. They see it as a barrier to their entry into the English-speaking North American mainstream. This sometimes causes resentment on the part of French Quebeckers. The problem for them is that the provincial birth rate is dropping below the number needed to maintain the current population. This means that fewer and fewer people will be around to support the culture of French Canada, unless the newcomers can be assimilated into it.

The Québec government has increased baby bonus money to encourage people to have larger families, but many Quebeckers consider the declining birth rate to be a serious problem for the future.

The St. Jean Baptiste Society sponsors a parade in Québec every June 24, which is a holiday in the province. The Society works to protect French language and culture.

Allophone refers to someone who speaks a language other than French or English.

United Nations Rules on Québec Sign Law

Read the article below about a business person in Québec who took his opposition to Bill 178, also known as the sign law, to the United Nations. In 1993, the eighteen people who serve on the UN Human Rights Committee in Geneva, Switzerland, ruled that Bill 178 was in violation of international standards of freedom of expression. They found that the sign law went against the International Covenant on Civil and Political Rights, a treaty signed by Canada. What do you think of his case?

What would you do if you were asked to remove a sign advertising your business because it was in a language not approved by the government?

To Gordon McIntyre, who refused to have his English sign taken down without a fight, the United Nations ruling that Québec's sign laws violate freedom of expression is a sweet victory.

"We're very happy, but we're kind of sad that we had to go above Canada's head," he said. "A plague on all their houses, the Liberals, the Conservatives and the NDP. We didn't have (them) to stand up for us."

Not everyone is so impressed. Some legal experts point out that the UN's ruling has no legal weight.

"The UN has no enforcement power, so it has the same moral suasion as an ombudsman," said Jack London of the University of Manitoba.

McIntyre complained to the United Nations Human Rights Committee in 1989, after an official from the Office de la langue français told him to remove the English outdoor sign on his Huntingdon funeral home in accordance with Québec's French-only sign law.

Then, McIntyre says, the federal government tried to block his complaint, and after the UN agreed to investigate in 1991, Canada created delays that tied up the case for months.

On Thursday, more than three years after he started, McIntyre got word from the UN: he had won.

McIntyre said a majority of the UN's Human Rights Committee had ruled that Canada had violated part of Article 19 of the International Convenant on Civil and Political Rights, which states that everyone has the right to freedom of expression.

The decision carries no legal weight, even though Canada is a signatory to the human rights covenant. However, it means Canada faces the embarrassment of a reprimand from the United Nations. If the sign law stands, Canada will face the further embarrassment of being a country where a UN human-rights ruling is flouted.

The English-rights lobby, Alliance Québec, and the Equality Party hailed the decision as a moral victory, a clear signal to the provincial government to scrap the sign law, which is currently up for review.

Jack London said the UN's ruling would not carry the same weight as its statements about human-rights violations in South Africa or Yugoslavia, because Canada's violation has caused far less human suffering. London said the ruling would not change any Québecer's mind about the sign law. The UN decision will only force the Québec government to change the sign law if it genuinely has the will to do so in the first place, he said.

McGill University law professor John Humphrey, who was instrumental in drafting the UN's Universal Declaration of Human Rights, said the ruling would carry great weight.

It puts a black mark on the reputations of both Québec and Canada. Canada is also to blame, he said, because Québec's Law 178 could not have been passed unless Premier Robert Bourassa

Although the United Nations is held in high regard around the world, countries are not bound by its decisions. Do you think Québec should change its sign law because of the ruling? Why or why not?

invoked the notwithstanding clause in the federal Constitution. That clause allows provinces to override the rights outlined in the Charter of Rights.

"If there has been a violation, it follows that the notwithstanding clause must also be in violation of international law," Humphrey said.

Making Choices

Should governments be able to make laws regulating the use of language? Why? Why not?

Human Rights

Like Canada's policy of multiculturalism, human rights policies in our country have changed over the years.

In the 1930s, provincial governments began to recognize the need for prohibiting discrimination. By the 1950s, they had started to pass laws that would ensure things like fair employment and equal pay for women.

In 1960, Prime Minister John Diefenbaker passed the Canadian Bill of Rights to protect many freedoms such as religion, speech, association, and freedom of the press. The Bill also recognized the rights of citizens to life, freedom, personal security, and the enjoyment of property.

In 1977, the Canadian government went further when it passed a law called the *Canadian Human Rights Act*. This act forbids

Non-governmental organizations such as Amnesty International work to uphold human rights around the world. What do you think would happen if there were no Human Rights Commissions in Canada?

discrimination based on the following factors: ethnic origin, colour, religion, gender, family status, marriage status, whether a person has a disability, and whether a person has ever been convicted of a crime or pardoned. The act also created the Canadian Human Rights Commission to hear complaints about discrimination. Many provinces followed the federal lead and set up their own commissions.

Both federal and provincial Human Rights Commissions hear many different kinds of complaints. In 1991, the Canadian Human Rights Commission had over 50 000 complaints filed, of which 1 000 were accepted as valid. Most of the complaints that were accepted were from people who had been discriminated against because of a disability. The second highest number of complaints came from people who had experienced discrimination because of their gender. Other complaints came from people who feel they are discriminated against because of their cultural background.

These women are protesting against discrimination. What other steps could they take? How do we make people who come from other countries aware of their rights as Canadian citizens?

Whose Rights are Right?

Sometimes individual rights come into conflict. People on each side of a dispute feel they have rights that are being violated. Read the case of Mrs. Wilson and decide if her rights were violated.

Should Mr. Pompei have the right to rent his property to anyone he chooses? Why or why not?

Mrs. Wilson, a Cree woman in her sixties, was looking for a house to rent. She heard that one was available in an ideal location close to the centre of Calgary. Mrs. Wilson and her daughters went to look at the house. Sure enough, there was a "For Rent" sign in the window. A woman next door told them that the owner was Antonio Pompei, who owned a bakery farther up the street.

Mrs. Wilson has great difficulty walking because she is almost blind, so she waited in the car while her daughters went along to the bakery. The daughters met with Mr. Pompei, who agreed to rent the house. However, the daughters wanted to look inside before they agreed to rent it. One of the bakery employees accompanied them to the house where he met Mrs. Wilson. All three women liked the house and returned to the bakery to tell Mr. Pompei that they would rent it.

When Mr. Pompei saw Mrs. Wilson, he promptly walked out of the bakery. He had not realized Mrs. Wilson was an Aboriginal person. Her daughters looked more like their father, who was of a different ethnic origin. The next day, Mrs. Wilson and her daughters returned to the bakery in an attempt to rent the house. Because of her blindness, Mrs. Wilson was helped out of the car and guided into the bakery by one of her daughters. Mr. Pompei told the women that the house was already rented to someone else.

The Wilsons suspected discrimination. As soon as they got home, Mrs. Wilson phoned Mr. Pompei. Without identifying herself, she asked about the house. He said it was still available. When Mrs. Wilson said who she was, Mr. Pompei lost his temper.

Mrs. Wilson complained to the Human Rights Commission. The investigating officer found that Mr. Pompei made incorrect assumptions about Mrs. Wilson because she had needed help from her daughter while walking. He did not know about her blindness. Mr. Pompei also said that the house was no longer available for rent when she phoned. However, the investigator discovered that the tenants who did eventually rent the house had not even seen it at the time of the phone call. They applied to rent it a full week after Mrs. Wilson tried to rent it.

Questions

1. Do you think Mr. Pompei would have rented this house to a blind woman who was not of Aboriginal origin?
2. What would you do if you were in Mrs. Wilson's position?
3. Have people you know ever been discriminated against because of their cultural background?

125

Chapter Review

7

What We Have Learned

The things we value as Canadians are embodied in certain symbols. These symbols may change over time as our culture changes. Attempts to use laws to preserve aspects of our culture have had mixed results. One basic Canadian value is that no one should be discriminated against because of their cultural background.

Talk About

Talk about how people are showing their understanding of multiculturalism today. Talk about cases of discrimination that you know about.

Questions

1. Why is the RCMP a Canadian symbol?
2. What purposes do symbols serve?
3. The Canadian flag has a maple leaf on it. Why was this symbol chosen, and what meaning does this image hold?

Activities

1. Create a timeline highlighting changes in Canada's flag or Canada's national anthem.
2. Describe a Canadian symbol that has changed in your lifetime.
3. Brainstorm Canadian symbols not mentioned in this chapter. Include them in a poster.

Challenges

1. Create a new symbol for Canada using an art form of your choice. Accompany your symbol with an explanation of why you created it.
2. Explain why other countries might admire and respect Canada's multicultural policies.
3. Choose a multicultural issue facing Canada today. Look for articles in the newspaper discussing this issue. Express your own viewpoint on the issue you have chosen.

Skill Builders

1. Review the case of Mrs. Wilson on page 125. With that example in mind, role-play the following scene. You own a boarding house with five rooms, four of which are rented to women. It is your only source of income. You advertise that you have a room for rent. A man calls and wants to rent the fifth room. You don't mind, but the women say they will move out if he moves in. How will you handle the situation? Should you have the right to refuse to rent the room to this man?
2. Develop your debating skills. First, write three arguments supporting the Québec government's position on Bill 101. Then write three arguments supporting the view that immigrants should be free to learn any language they want. Set up a formal debate in your class between the two sides.

Multiculturalism Into the Future

8 Imagining Tomorrow

In this book, you have learned how, over the years, people of various cultural backgrounds have come to live in Canada. The Aboriginal Peoples were once the only inhabitants of Canada. They were joined by French and British colonists, who came because of the opportunities available in the fur and fish trades. Gradually, people from other lands arrived, escaping poverty or persecution in their own countries, and seeking a new life in a new land. People from every country in the world have come to live in Canada and call it home.

> We do not want to have in Canada a little France, a little England, a little Italy or a little Russia. We want in Canada a great country for all the people in Canada, for all the ethnic groups in our country. Through that channel we will achieve unity and we will reinforce our position in the whole world.
>
> —Real Caouette, Créditiste leader, 1971.

Everyday, people from all over the world come to Canada to start new lives.

As a result of all of this immigration, Canada is a country of traditions from many cultures. These traditions are passed on from generation to generation in the form of stories, customs, festivals, ways of dressing, and ways of thinking. Many of these traditions are maintained by newcomers to Canada who feel comfortable with their familiar way of doing things. Other traditions are changed or, in some cases, abandoned as people adopt new ways of doing things. This is the process of becoming Canadian.

Newcomers to Canada are not forced to make changes to their traditions. They are not told that they must behave in a certain way when they become Canadians. Newcomers are free to retain their traditions if they choose. This is the cornerstone of the government policy of multiculturalism.

The policy of multiculturalism encourages Canadians to keep up their cultural traditions. You have learned that not everyone agrees that this is a good idea. Critics of the multiculturalism policy worry that it creates divisions in Canadian society. The following is a summary of some of the arguments you have read in this book.

Think About

How would you answer each of these questions?

Do cultural differences weaken Canadian unity?

Yes.

How can we have a strong nation if people maintain their own cultures instead of becoming Canadian?

No.

We are stronger because we have learned to live with our differences. People can have pride in their cultural backgrounds and still be good Canadians.

Does keeping our ethnic traditions cause too many problems?

Yes.

The more differences there are, the more problems they produce. There are always misunderstandings when people of different backgrounds mix.

No.

The benefits of diversity far outweigh the problems. As we get used to living with people from other cultures, most of the problems will disappear anyway.

Is it a good idea to learn the language of your ancestors?

Yes.
You will be able to better understand your own background. Anyway, learning more than one language is always a good idea.

No.
You only need to know French or English to get along in Canada. Learning another language is a waste of time.

Should ethnic groups maintain their traditions?

Yes.
Ethnic groups from many places built this country. Their traditions are part of Canadian history.

No.
When people move to a new country, they should adapt to the ways of that country. They should give up the traditions of their native country.

These are very important questions for Canada's future. As Canadian citizens, it is your responsibility to think about these issues and become involved in building the future of this country. Each one of you can make a difference. Your attitudes and ideas will influence the kind of country Canada will become. Everyone must take part in building a strong nation that truly reflects the values, visions, hopes, and ideals of its people.

You have learned in this book that multiculturalism is a government policy. You have also learned that it is a way of describing Canadian society. Canada is a place where people of many backgrounds meet, mingle, and make a life together. Every individual has the same rights and freedoms, no matter where they came from originally.

People of all backgrounds must learn to live together if Canadian society is going to succeed. There is no room for attitudes such as racism and discrimination that divide people instead of bringing them together. Throughout your life, you will meet many people of different cultures with diverse backgrounds. How well you get along together will influence the kind of society Canada becomes.

The following are three visions of the future from three Canadians of very diverse backgrounds:

Building Bridges Between Cultures

by Sangeeta Virmani

CCG newsletter, May 1993

At our school, you have a chance to see the beauty to be experienced when bridges unite cultures. Here you are respected for who you are, not what you wear and not what you look like. Just a little change today can make a huge difference tomorrow.

Margaret Mead said, "Real culture lives by sympathies and admirations, not by dislikes and disdains." Every day, I mix with students from many cultures. I delight in learning about their traditions and feel privileged to share them. I have expanded my mind by listening to different philosophies and values.

Millions of immigrants have been victims of persecution, suffered hunger, been denied adequate medical aid, and lived in bloodshed. Haven't they sacrificed enough? Would you also have them become totally assimilated into our culture? Would you shut your mind to what we can gain by learning more of their culture, their traditions, their philosophies and ideas?

We must eliminate the racial discrimination that is a product of our ignorance.

Construction, not destruction, is the answer. Build bridges, join cultures—don't destroy them.

132

Let's Stop Racism

by Phyllis Littletent

CCG newsletter, May 1993

"They say that the wheels of justice
They grind slowly,
Yes, we know...
and what they grind
is human beings...
The humanity
of the victims
who get caught
in its jaw..."

These words of wisdom were spoken by Art Solomon, an Ojibwa spiritual leader.

If I could make a difference, everyone would be treated with dignity and respect, regardless of their race.

Yes, there's something to sing about,
Tune up a string about,
Call out in chorus or quietly hum
Of a land that is young
With a ballad that's still unsung
Sharing the promise of great things to come. . . ."
    —from "Something to Sing About"

133

If I Could See Tomorrow...

by Nathanael Amacker

Think About

What images of Canada's future have been presented in these three selections?

This selection is from the first-prize speech at the 4th annual public-speaking competition in conjunction with the International Day for the Elimination of Racial Discrimination, March 1992. The theme was "Multiculturalism Works—It Defeats Racism."

Relax a moment, close your eyes if you wish, and try to picture the world of tomorrow through my eyes. I want you to experience the world of tomorrow as I think, hope and dream the future will become. If all creatures were valued and respected, racism would be just another skeleton in the closet, hidden away for all time.

We're now heading for school, everything is crystal clear and bright. Feel the difference in the atmosphere. The very atmosphere feels friendly. It gives us the urge to dance, jump for joy, feel free. Can you feel the difference? Friendly smiles are on everyone's face. There's the caretaker happily raising the flag. The secretary is busy registering some new students from Romania. Now look at the playground. People of all nationalities are playing together; there are no fights, no hateful words, instead there is the joyful sound of laughter. Girls, a mixture of races, are learning the intricacy of Chinese skipping, and some other students are enjoying the taste of moon-cake. Just look at how green the trees are! Breathe deeply and savour the fresh clean air. Notice the flowers basking in the sun. You are now in a perfect world. There is no need for laws in this world, everyone is too happy to break them anyway. It is a perfect world—it's as if we've put all the pieces of a giant puzzle together...

Our future, our tomorrow, is still an unknown quantity. We, everyone in this room, have the power of making my dream come true. If we sit back and let life happen to us—well then, we deserve to live in a nightmare. Fortunately our actions today can, they really can, defeat racism and create a world that looks like my dream. See my dream—believe it possible—get out and help me achieve it. Start now—make a friend of everyone you meet. Celebrate the differences and link arms with people from other cultures. Your life will be richer and the world will be a better place. Multiculturalism really works—it defeats racism—it really does.

A Last Note

You all have hopes and dreams about the future. Every day you work toward your goals. What you choose to study in school, how you conduct yourself with others, the attitudes you have toward school, parents, friends, and family are all part of a foundation that you are building on as you grow up.

As you learned in this book, multiculturalism is both a way of describing society, and an official government policy. It is an idea that has developed over many years. But this does not mean that it might not change as society changes. That is for you and other Canadians to decide.

In your own life, your behaviour and attitudes are constantly being tested. A "bad" attitude usually gets a response that makes you change. A "good" attitude is often rewarded by a smile, a pat on the back, or by some other mark of approval that encourages you to keep on acting that way. In the same way, Canadians must test their attitudes about multiculturalism. We must continue to ask ourselves whether our policies are serving us well as a society, whether they are helping to make Canada a better place to live. This is a never-ending task. When we see things we do not like, we try to change them through citizen participation, by asking tough questions, and by working hard to make changes.

Reflect on the following:
- Before 1918, women were not allowed to vote.
- Inuit people only received the right to vote in 1950.
- Aboriginal People living on reserves did not receive the vote until 1960.
- In 1970, the federal voting age dropped from twenty-one to eighteen years.

1. What do these facts say about the value of each group to Canadian society?
2. How does not being able to vote affect a person's ability to participate in Canadian society?

We can try to change things we do not like through citizen participation in special interest groups. The group pictured here is fighting for equality in education.

You have learned that multiculturalism promotes sharing. It encourages you to appreciate and respect the way others live, even if it is different from the way you live. Multiculturalism promotes the opening of minds and the building of bridges.

You have read about many new factors that have changed Canadian society. People from many cultures have arrived, bringing their diverse traditions with them. Canadian traditions have changed as people have borrowed ideas from one another. There have been difficulties, but there have also been great rewards as people have learned to live together as Canadians.

This book began with the suggestion that the way people live together is like an orchestra. Every person brings a special talent and has a particular job to do. Together they combine to make beautiful

"music." The music, however, does not stay the same. Today, computers have become instruments used to compose and perform. New styles of music, such as rap, continue to appear. You may like all types of music, or you may just prefer one type–country, jazz, rock, classical– over any other. In Canada, laws protect our right to make choices such as what music we like, where we worship, or how we express ourselves.

Through looking at the past and present experiences of Canadians, *Multiculturalism in Canada: Images and Issues* discusses many of the issues surrounding the rights and freedoms of Canadians, and the implications of Canada as a multicultural nation. We have learned that the more educated Canadian citizens are about the issues Canada has faced in the past, the better we will be able to deal with the challenges that Canada will face in the future. We are all responsible for making sure that Canada, the "community of communities," as well as all Canadians, live up to our potential.

Has multiculturalism fulfilled its promise?

Multiculturalism has been the most important idea introduced in Canada in the past twenty years. It has shaped Canada as a nation, and will continue to promote Canada as a respected country.

It's still too soon to tell whether multiculturalism has been good or bad for Canada. The jury is still out…

Multiculturalism has not fulfilled all of its promises. Unless we change our ways of thinking about multiculturalism in the future, all we will have in Canada is a bunch of different groups of people living together under different cultural roles and laws who will never form a Canadian culture.

Multiculturalism has helped us build bridges between cultures and not walls. It will be the way in which we will eliminate racism in the future.

Multiculturalism is getting out of hand. It's too much of a good thing. If we continue to look at our differences rather than our similarities, our country will be very fractured in the future. Why is government telling us who we should be?

Making Choices

What is your opinion of the future of multiculturalism in Canada? Write a speech. Deliver your speech to your classmates, role-playing the part of a person trying to get elected to Parliament. Would your speech change depending on the type of people in the audience? Explain why or why not.

137

What Have We Learned

As Canada changes, so do attitudes toward multiculturalism. Looking toward the future, there are many issues to be faced, and many choices to be made. Every Canadian has a role to play in determining the future. It is both a right and a responsibility to help shape this future.

Talk About

Has multiculturalism touched your life as a Canadian?

Questions

1. What role do institutions play in multiculturalism?
2. Under what circumstances could multiculturalism become troublesome?
3. Should Canadians continue with multiculturalism in the same manner as they do today? Why? Why not?
4. As Canadian citizens, what are our responsibilities to Canada? In the present? In the future?

Activities

1. Write a "To Do" list of things every Canadian should do to be a good citizen.
2. As a class, create a poster or mural illustrating Canadians building bridges of understanding.
3. Write a poem or song about Canada and the future of multiculturalism.

Challenges

1. Brainstorm a list of possible events that might influence Canada's multiculturalism policy in the future.
2. Think about what you will be doing in the year 2025. What will a typical day in your life look like? What contributions will you be making as a citizen? What will your community look like? Express your ideas about the future in writing, or another art form such as music, painting, drama, or dance.

Skill Builders

1. Write the following headings in your notebook and complete a personal inventory on multiculturalism:

A Personal Inventory on How I Can be Involved in the Future of Multiculturalism in Canada	
How can I influence those who make political decisions?	How can I change my own actions?
How can I influence people in my own community?	How can I express my views?
How can I find out more?	What other actions can I take?

For example, if you wish to influence people who make political decisions, you might write to a local politician, or invite one to your school, or you might even decide to get involved in the youth wing of a political party in your area.

Form into small groups and brainstorm all the possibilities under each of the six headings. Discuss them with the whole class.

2. Develop your essay writing skills by writing about the future of multiculturalism in Canada. As part of the essay, try to answer the following questions:
   a. How can we determine if Canada has done well in managing multiculturalism?
   b. Has multiculturalism made Canada a better place to live?
   c. Should we be following the same road into the future? If not, what road should we take?
   d. What lies in store for the future of multiculturalism in Canada?

139

Index